Microdosing Magic
A Psychedelic Spellbook

Tom Hatsis

Cover design/intro art/page graphics: Gwyllm Llwydd
Magic graphs and sacred geometry: Vanessa Tutka
Edited by: Eden Woodruff

Contents

AD LECTOREM

Until this time all my professional focus remained squarely within the realm of psychedelic history. But as I toured the country speaking in support of my book *The Witches' Ointment*, the conversations with those interested in my work started shifting away from history and towards my personal magical practices and philosophies. I was often asked dose sizes, magical techniques, potion ingredients, and the like. Having used these tools since my late teens, I had half a lifetime of trial and error to figure things out and plenty of safety instructions to share.

It's obvious why my audience asks me more about psychedelic use than about psychedelic history as of late. Newer (and unbiased) research keeps demonstrating that moderate psychedelic use, far from harming responsible users, can actually compliment a healthy and active lifestyle. As we rediscover the true history of these extraordinary plants and fungi—that they have been used for thousands of years to heal the emotional, physical, mental, and spiritual needs of countless people—many of our contemporaries, tired of the side-effects of pharmaceuticals, are turning to these timeless medicines.

Some of us, however, who thankfully do not need (at least not yet) to rely on pharmaceuticals have still found a smidgen of personal enlightenment from such Goddess-sends like mushrooms, cacti, cannabis, 5-MeO DMT, and a host of equally reliable synthetic compounds.

But how exactly do we use the insights of the psychedelic experience? How do we bring that magic into our lives *daily* without needing to take a high dose of say, LSD, every several months? I offer this short spellbook as a possible start to dealing with those questions.

Microdosing: if yes, then who?

While the reports of microdosing have by and large come back as safe and positive, some people may be sensitive to these kinds of substances. For example, if you take Serotonin Reuptake Inhibitors (SSRI) or anti-depressants there exists the possibility that you will experience Serotonin Syndrome, an over-stimulation of serotonin that leads to symptoms like sweating, increased body heat, and diarrhea. The online resource microdosingpsychedelics. com provides an invaluable list of various drug interactions that would be well for anyone to consider before putting anything in their body.

Additionally, even if not taking SSRIs or other pharmaceuticals, anyone with mental illness (or a family history of it) should seriously weigh every option and speak to a trusted physician before taking even a microdose. In fact, a good way to think about microdosing can be summed up by Lakota Shaman Hawkeye Clark, "if you wouldn't take a psychedelic dose, do not start microdosing either."[1]

For those of you in good mental and physical health with an interest in microdosing, the answer to the question of who should microdose is probably *you*. But since I really don't know I will say a few things about the intention of this short psychedelic spellbook and leave the decision up to you:

1. If you are unsure whether to start microdosing then this spellbook is not for you. This spellbook is for the person who has decided to microdose and wants to get the most out of the practice.

2. This spellbook is also for those who are already microdosing and want to explore new approaches to it.

3. It is for those who have a goal and want to use microdosing and magic to accompany and enhance the process.

1. Hawkeye, pers. comm.

4. It is a spellbook of magical fundamentals for those who know there is enchantment in the world and desire to know how to access it.

Make no mistake, psychedelics are *tools.* A hammer does not teach a builder how to make a table. Microdosing without a plan is like asking a hammer how to build a table.

For some, microdosing has been used as a way to *tolerate* an otherwise uneventful and joyless life. Psychedelic researcher Paul Austin says that such a route (i.e., microdosing solely to tolerate life) will rarely result in lasting benefits. I agree with Austin, but only to a point; microdosing *alone* to cure an intolerable life will doubtful lead to lasting results. On the other paw, if you plan to use microdosing to *better* a life that you are sick of merely *tolerating*, if you know you want *something* but are not sure what it is or how to get it, then you just may find this silly little volume impractically practical.

This short spellbook is not meant to change you in some radical way that I, as the author, deem appropriate. Instead, this is a collection of magical techniques designed and used by yours truly to help me overcome crippling self-doubt, own my focus, rekindle my childlike wonder, and change my life for the better. Also, since I think it's important to outline why I do the things I do (and hold the beliefs I hold), some of my thoughts on history and philosophy have found their way into these pages as well.

Mostly this book is about discovering just how magical you are.

Even more mostly, it's about displaying that magic as a natural extension of yourself.

Even much more mostly, it's about using microdosing to achieve those ends.

.1.

STAR STUFF
The Basics of Magic

Who am I?

Why are we here?

What is my purpose?

These questions, and many more like them, will be ignored in this book.

Instead, I have set aside, dressed, marinated, and grilled the following pages not to answer questions but to outline how I used microdoses of mushrooms and magical techniques to create the kind of life that works for me. We all have this ability. But sometimes when we get caught up in the disorders of modern life we can forget to utilize it. However, once each of us does, such questions like those posed above crumble and fall away from concern.

That is the power of microdosing magic.

Magic animates us all. Our minds cannot escape magic any more than our lungs can escape breathing air. It is an immaterial ability we possess no different from that other immaterial ability we possess called "thought." Magic is a kind of thinking that tethers us all to the Realm of Possibility. Once there, we have the ability to make things better for ourselves by considering our circumstances within the occult traditions housed in that magical Realm.

Now I'm not totally clear on the science behind this, but magic seems to be the result of physical bodies (us) containing residual immaterial forces of the universe as it exploded and then expanded into whatever existed before space and time. According to the late great astrophysicist and cannabis enthusiast Carl Sagan (who is totally clear on the science behind this), "The cosmos is within us. We are made of star-stuff. We are a way for the universe to know itself." In other words, we are the shattered chips of cosmic wonder ricocheting off space and time since the initial Big Bang.

We are, in fact, microdoses of its magic. ☺
Whodathunk?!?!

Magical forces are not made of consciousness. They see nothing; they judge us naught. But they do respond to stimulation. These forces are not supernatural. In fact, they form the basis of naturalism as we understand it. We can see signs of this glorious natural magic all around us— from the moon's effect on tides and menstruation to other marvels like gravity and farting.

As individual reflections of the cosmos wishing to know itself, we come equipped with tools: Three Spiritual Forces (Emotion, Intellect, and Will); and, as part of our natural evolution in physical bodies, we also enjoy One Material Force (Action). These Four Gifts, at base, begin as either love or hate, altruism or narcissism, creation or destruction, and everything in between. Magic puts the Four Gifts into your hands so that they do not control you. Honing the natural powers of the Four Gifts grants you access to the Realm of Possibility.

Aligning the Four Gifts via magic (usually referred to as "flow state") to tap the Realm of Possibility is akin to floating adrift in an Ocean. The Ocean (The Realm) has *no idea* that you are awash in its bosom. *You*, however, are quite aware of the wetness of your body, the smell of sea salt in the air, and the pressure on your limbs as you move through the rolling waves. The Ocean does not judge you; in fact, it doesn't know who you are and doesn't even have the capacity to care.

And yet, the Ocean produces life, all the while unaware that it is doing so. While the Ocean is not conscious, it breeds the very conscious beings that will displace it. There are crustaceans, sea mammals like whales, jellyfish, and other aquatic life. As for you, you are conscious and therefore have some options. You can move your arms and splash the water, kick your legs, or even cup your hands and move the waves from your right side to

3

your left. You can drink the water if you choose or reject it as unpotable. You can control the water with no guilt that you are not receiving any consent from it. Or you can do nothing at all—simply float on by. The Ocean reacts not out of spite, or love, or pain but merely to the ebbs and flows of its own tidal creations: seaweed, higher-cognitive aquatic life, and *you*. For such is the nature of Ocean.

It is your job to harness your magic and *swim*.

For such is the nature of you.

Operating our magic to tap the Realm of Possibility works something like floating in the Ocean; the tides of both (our magic and the Realm) are always turning. When we do not recognize these mechanisms we remain detached from a very powerful tool at our disposal.[1] Since things like lying, theft, violence, and other not-niceties (those dealings within the sphere of the Four Gifts) confuse the conscious-less cosmos with toxic stimulation (to which it will nonetheless respond), we can unwittingly create spiritual havoc with our thoughts and actions (i.e. mindlessly splashing and kicking in the Ocean). A vibrant and active magical consciousness results in a delightful backstroke.

And why is owning your unique slice of magic so valuable? Because, if Sagan is correct, then as a tiny slice of a universe that wishes to know itself, you are responsible for your life, philosophies, spiritual ideas, and the like. Trying to change yourself at your core or adopt someone else's magical perspective denies the universe a boundless

---

1. See the second principle of magic, below.

piece of itself. You cannot swim for a drowning person. Therefore, what makes you *you* is the treasure itself. The more you own *you*, the more magical you are.

In this short spellbook, we will be working with the Four Gifts that exist as natural extensions of the magical cosmos: the Three Spiritual Forces (Emotion, Intellect, Will), and the One Material Force, our inheritance from physical reality (Action). When we lose sight of the inherent powers in our Four Gifts we create unneeded (and usually avoidable) discord.

An easy way to keep the Four Gifts in right relation is through microdosing magic.

PSYCHEDELIC MAGIC

Magic is a mentality, a way to recognize and enjoy the Four Gifts, while psychedelics stimulate the mind, boosting our ability to recognize the daily wonder in life and take full advantage of it. As more and more people discover the natural benefits of microdosing, I wanted to offer a quick spellbook outlining the magical supplements of that endeavor. Don't get me wrong, microdosing by itself is a fantastic revitalization tool. The beauty of the psychedelic alone is the remarkable way it boosts energy, creativity, optimism, and combats depression.

But you could be getting so much more out of it!

Indeed, many people who microdose take their dose in the morning and go about their day regularly. This approach champions the psychedelic only, without doing much work to compliment the dose cycle.[2] This is fine, of course. But just as mushrooms are medicinal they are *also* magical, and to ignore the magical side of the mushroom is to only receive half the benefits and blessings from them.

I liken microdosing and magic to a healthy diet and exercise. Both are fine without the other, but both are also *so much more* when conjoined. Or consider the following: because of the amount of touring I do, my friend Jim installed a hydrogen gas unit in my car. Hydrogen gas units are truly a Goddess-send; they double your gas mileage. I am not sure of the chemistry or the engineering that takes place, but my understanding of it is this: when you fill up your car's gas tank you actually only use 50% of the gas itself. The other 50% is burned up in emissions. These hydrogen gas units convert those usually burnt up emissions into hydrogen fuel, thus ensuring you get 100% of the gas in your tank.

Microdosing magic works something like that: microdosing alone will definitely put gas in your tank, so to speak. But microdosing magic will ensure that you utilize 100% of your tank's capacity.

Magic 101

If you are unfamiliar with magic, I offer three basic principles that I have found useful:

1. *All magic is done to affect future outcomes.*
Odd as it sounds, that's as simple as it gets. Recently a

---

2. For setting and maintaining a dose cycle, see chapter 3.

friend of mine shared a post on social media that went something like this: "people always say that if they had a time machine they would go back to the past to make some change that affected them in a positive way today. But they never think of taking those same actions today to affect the future." This was of course met with such comments like "mind blown" and "interesting perspective." I informed my friend that *that* has been the magician's credo since time immemorial! The incident made me realize that perhaps many people have an erroneous idea about what magic is all about. Magic is not some mysterious endeavor engaged by guys sporting slicked black hair tied in a stubby ponytail, claw rings, and a dyed-black goatee.[3] Magic is simply about affecting future outcomes in your favor.

2. *You are always making magic.*

Yes, everything you do, every Action you take, everything you say has a ripple effect in the world. This is why honing your relationship with the Four Gifts is so important. The more ethical and moral you hold your Intellect, Emotion, and Will the less you have to worry about repercussions; this frees your mind to engage its magical technologies.

3. *The more playful and curious (i.e., childlike) you are the more magical you become.*

Children are the most magical creatures there are (besides cats). Comedian Jerry Seinfeld once remarked that when

---

3. Okay, *sometimes* it's that.

7

kids dress up as superheroes for Halloween they do not see their outfits as "costumes" but rather as "options." Instead of stressing this point here I have saved a deeper discussion of this principle's importance for Chapter 9.

Let's put these three principles into a single sentence: since magic is about affecting future outcome, and you are always making magic anyway, the goodness and efficacy of which relies on your ability to reconnect with childlike wonder, then you may as well reinstall your childlike wonder and put your magic to good use. This is the power of intention-based magic.

Now, when I say "intention-based," I am not referring to some kind of gobbledygook one will find between the pages of *The Secret*. Such books offer not magical thinking but rather miracle thinking, and miracle thinking stops you from thinking magically. Sometimes magical thinking is confused with miracle thinking. Since they are hardly the same thing I wish to address their differences here because, like medicinal mushrooms that grow side by side with poisonous ones, miracle thinking is equally deadly to the magical mind.

Miracle thinking is wish fulfillment.

Wish fulfillment is the limousine liberal's answer to the conservative's "thoughts and prayers." Wish fulfillment is not a recipe for any kind of real, *authentic* change. It is miracle thinking. Miracle thinking is a trap. It is the lottery. You are not going to win the lottery; you will not perform miracles.

In some rare but extreme cases, I've watched this kind of activity bring out less desirable traits in otherwise good people. I have literally heard one of these miracle-thinking New Agers say that impoverished people simply have "bad money karma" and needed to refocus their negative energy "meditating on good money."

What a terrible thing to say. That is not magical thinking. It is miracle thinking and we are all too magical to require miracles.

Magical thinking works within circumstances.

Setting the intention

Since most of this book discusses things you can do (if you so choose), the question of free Will, with regards to any philosophy or theosophy, ought to be addressed.

Do we have free Will? While some say *yes* and others say *no*, the honest answer is: *sort of.* It would appear that we have Will within the confines of our circumstances. Will is, after all, one of the Three Spiritual Forces we inherited from our origins in the stars. Our evolved bodies, however, limit our celestial Will's range to material Action. For example, I can freely drive to Seattle, Washington, from where I am (Portland, Oregon) should it be my Will, but I cannot freely drive to Shanghai, China, because cars don't work over water (to say nothing of travel expenses). If it is my Will to drive to Seattle today, so mote it be; if it is my Will to drive to Shanghai today, so no it be. Setting an unrealistic intention (driving to China today) will only serve to disrupt one of the Four Gifts, my Will.

Magic takes time, so if you expect instant results (i.e., miracles) no amount of psychedelics or magic can help you. The hardest part is remembering to trust the magic. Expecting instant results is not magical thinking, it is miracle thinking. Magic is *work*. It is not lip service to the "Universe" in hope of a future reward.

You have to set *realistic* intentions, do the work, and let your magic guide you.

WHAT'S THE MIND?

Oftentimes when we encounter a troubled friend, loved one, or even stranger our default question is "what's the matter?" Such an organization of words would lead one to erroneously think that matter creates mind—*quite the opposite*! It is, in fact, our minds that create matter. Thus, a better question than "what's the matter" would be "what's the mind?" As philosopher Sam Harris noted "Any athlete knows that certain kinds of pain can be pleasurable. The burn of lifting weights, for instance, would be excruciating if it were a symptom of terminal illness. But because it is associated with health and fitness, most people find it enjoyable."[4] Simple stings from life can be changed through nothing more than altering one's mindset.

This is not to say that one shouldn't grieve over loss. We are all human, so this principle of "what's the mind?" is not license to be cold in the face of tragedy. Telling a friend whose dog got hit by a car to "just change

4. Sam Harris, *Waking Up*, pg. 16.

your perspective, dude" isn't spiritual or magical; it's just an insensitive dick move. Further, this is not to say that if you only "think positively" bad things won't happen to you. We must all process the (un)foreseen hiccups in life, so this "what's the mind" principle is not a spiritual-bypass. It is rather a way to remember the power you have over the *small* things—over the little peeves that build up overtime that inevitably release as regrettable Action.

The best demonstration of mind over matter can be experienced personally, by you, right now. Read this short exercise (*italicized*) and then put the book down and try it before reading forward (no peeking!):

Close your eyes and imagine you are walking through your local grocery store. Really visualize the store (I will discuss visualization below), noting the tiles on the floor, the crates of vegetables, other shoppers—everything! Approach a bin of bright red apples and take one from the bunch. Feel the smooth skin of the apple in your hands, hold it close to your nose and inhale its appley smell. Hold your focus here until you can really see and smell the apple. Take a bite. Taste it. Continue walking past the other produce until you reach the lemon bin. Take one of those little yellow suns out of the bunch. Roll your fingers across the top, feeling the rough skin of the fruit. To your left you see a knife sitting on a wooden cutting board. Put the lemon on the board and cut it into small pieces. Place one of those bits in your mouth and suck on it. Stay there for 30 seconds; sucking on the lemon ...

... Your lips are puckering aren't they? You are having a physiological reaction to the lemon and yet there is no lemon in sight. *That* is just a small sample of your mind's ability to create your reality.[5]

Now that we know we are magical and awesome star-stuff that can do cool shit like this, the natural question arises: how do we develop it more?! The two most tried and true techniques of using your conscious mind to manifest physical realities are meditation and visualization—in that order.

MEDITATION AND VISUALIZATION

Meditation is the practice of learning the patterns and designs of your mind, offering a way to develop more insight into moment to moment existence. The idea behind meditation is to be aware of the fact that you are thinking by paying close attention to what flows in and out of your consciousness. Consider this: we are thinking *all* day, but rarely are we paying attention to it! When we meditate we are actively listening to our thoughts.

The results from meditation are typically positive. Most meditators experience better emotional states and focus, while also seeing a decrease in depression, anxiety, and stress. But just like psychedelics, meditation should not be seen as a "cure all." While our popular Western

---

5. This "mind revelation" adapted from Bob Hoffman, *No One is to Blame*, p. 63.

notions see meditators as unquestioningly "enlightened," there are many, in fact, who qualify as pretentious assholes. Mahatma Gandhi would meditate for two hours some days; this did nothing to curb his insufferable racism.[6] Likewise, Buddhist scripture includes a story of Siddhartha Gautama (who later became the Buddha) in one of his past lives. In this particular incarnation Siddhartha lived as Prince Vessantara, a man who was *so enlightened* that he sold his wife and children into slavery as a demonstration of his pious detachment from earthly goods.[7] Even meditating for seven weeks couldn't stop the Buddha from considering his wife "property."

These are extreme examples, of course. I mention them only as a reminder that you are probably already more enlightened than those considered "holy" by popular standards. And that if they could master meditation, so can you! For most, meditation has proven a powerful route to clarity and overall positive mental health by slowing and diminishing the amount of thoughts that constantly roll through our minds.

It achieves this by working the Three Spiritual Forces in the following ways:

<u>*Emotional Awareness* (*Emotion*)</u> – there was a time when modern life had reduced me to a skin-bag of nerves.

---

6 . See Ashwin Desai and Goolam Vahed, *The South African Gandhi: Stretcher-Bearer of Empire* (CA: Stanford University Press, 2015).
7. Robert M. Ellis, *The Trouble with Buddhism* (Lulu.com, 2011), pg. 89; *cf* Minor Anthologies of the Pali Canon, Part III.

Nothing more. My life consisted of a rat race, followed by a rut, followed by a rat race, followed by a rut. Such a cycle results in low-vibe, emotionally-drained output that eventually dies in apathy and sloth. Therefore, Emotion plays a large role not just in our day to day lives, but can really affect us over the long-haul of life through the creation of negative patterns. Emotions have the power to elevate or disrupt our greatest intentions.

Anxiety (*Intellect*) – When we are caught in a rat race followed by a rut on constant loop we are not living in right relation with our creative faculties—out Intellect. This causes unneeded stress, which only serves to reinforce negative Emotion. Remember – *you are always making magic.* If you are stressed, such will be the outcome of your magical returns.

Detachment from Addictive Behaviors (*Will*) – For some, meditation has proven mildly effective for calming habits and cravings. This most likely has to do with lowering stress. We more often reach for our cigarettes, beers, and blunts after a hard day. As such, if we are able to stay peacefully within the moment when disturbances arise we will naturally lower our overall anxiety, and coping habits, during the day. The more we abstain from addictive behaviors, the stronger our Will grows.

The ability to achieve a meditative state of mind is *crucial*

14

to microdosing magic. If you are an experienced meditator, feel free to skip to the next subchapter. But if meditating is new to you, consider doing the following:

1. Find a quiet place.

2. Sit totally erect in a comfortable position. While I am sometimes jealous of those who cross their legs (lotus position) and do the whole swami thing while meditating, I am a kitty of a different breed: I like to sit in a chair, feet flat on the floor, shoulder-width apart. Works just as well. ☺

3. Close your eyes.

4. Focus on your breath, paying attention to the space between inhale and exhale. Count silently to four as you inhale, hold for four seconds, and release again for four seconds. Eventually cease counting and stay solely on your breath as much as possible.

5. Think of your ass sitting on the floor or chair as well as any other physical sensations. *Don't* scratch any itches …. okay, try not to as long as possible.

6. Pay attention to your thoughts. We are bombarded with so much stimuli during the day but we seldom take note of the fact that we *are* thinking.

7. Stay *there*. In the present moment.

I learned how to do this overtime. The easiest and most direct way to develop this contemplative awareness is to meditate (focus, as best as you can, on nothing but your breath) for two minutes a day, every day, for one week. Come next Monday meditate for four minutes every day of the week. The week after that, take it up to six minutes a day (and so on). Once you've made it to ten minutes a day, restart at two minutes and work your way up to ten again. It takes time to develop your meditative awareness, but the rewards of coupling it with microdosing, visualization (discussed below), and other magic techniques, I think you'll agree, are worth the effort.

One does not always have to find a strictly quiet place to meditate. Sometimes I like going to a wooded area or a park, closing my eyes, and focusing on all the different sounds of the forest. The key is to differentiate between what you feel (the ground, the wind, any comfort or discomfort, itches) and the different sounds (birds chirping, rustles in the underbrush, airplanes flying overhead, etc.). You can even do this if you live or work on a busy street: try to distinguish every sound from the cacophony—the construction crane, the chirping birds, the honking of car horns, conversations outside your window, etc.

Meditating allows the prefrontal cortex to grow new connections. This aids problem solving, memory, language, motor function, impulse control, and social grace. Your mindfulness grows as well. Mindfulness is simply awareness of your thoughts, feelings, sensations, and mood; it is also an awareness of those same qualities as observed in others. In many ways that's what meditation is about: observation. But observation free from judgment. Your mind becomes a switch that you can turn on and off, which slows thought and therefore combats unnecessary judgments; it is now free to visualize.

NOW YOU SEE IT!

Visualization works much like the lemon "mind revelation" above. The idea is to create a conscious theater of your desires. Instead of worrying about a job interview, for example, visualize yourself in the interview. Aren't you kicking ass? After all, your resume is stellar, you are dressed professionally, and—goddamn it—you are likable! See yourself knocking the interview questions out of the park. In fact, this works really well if you are familiar with the person who will be interviewing you. See her grilling you in your mind.

The key to visualization is *detail*. You want to be as meticulous as possible while envisioning the scene. You want to see *everything* in your magical imagination. The best way to prepare for visualization is to meditate for 20-30 minutes first. Then, once the mind is satisfactorily quieted, shift to visualizing, beginning with the body; close your eyes and "look" at you arms, hands, and fingers in front of you. See your torso, thighs, knees, calves, socks and sneakers. From there, move the visualizing into the "outside" world within your inner magical awareness.

HOW TO BUILD A PSYCHEDELICALLY MAGICAL MIND

Recently professor of pharmacology at Purdue University, David Nichols, hypothesized that microdosing works as a stimulant by activating dopamine pathways and exciting the central cortex.[8] This is the very area that, if damaged, meditation helps rebuild!

Staying with the meditation→visualization technique, this procedural order is crucial for getting the most out of microdosing magic. I find that microdosing magic is best done in the morning. Indeed, I have just woken up and haven't terrorized myself with social media yet. I haven't sat in traffic yet, or got cut off by a speeding car while riding my bike. The rackets of life haven't ping-ponged me back and forth yet.

Dreams are still fresh, stirring in the morning air.

Mushrooms tend to start kicking in for most people about 20 - 30 minutes after ingesting them—roughly the same amount of time it takes to reach a meditative state! And so I tend to wake up, eat my dose (any size), and meditate immediately for that first half hour. Then, as the mushrooms and I merge, I switch to visualization, allowing

8. Erin Brodwin, "The Truth about Microdosing, which Involves Taking Tiny Amounts of Psychedelics like LSD," *Business Insider* (30 January 2017); accessed via: businessinsider.com.

the fungus to do what it does best: ignite the creative imagination. These post-meditative moments are most magically powerful due to the amount of effort it takes to control the visualization once the mind starts firing from the mushrooms. It is quite the exercise—like adding additional weights to a barbell. This is not an easy process, but it is a worthwhile pursuit. For it is *here*, visualizing with a quieted mind against the push and pull of the mushroom, that we harness the fungus' magic, energy, and wisdom.

It is *here* where we begin to unravel the mysteries of potential in the Realm of Possibility.

It is *here* where we begin unlocking the secrets of microdosing magic. ☺

.2.

MUSHROOM ALCHEMY AND NEUROGENESIS
ANCIENT MEDICINE, MODERN SYMPTOMS

While a veritable psychedelic smorgasbord awaits any seeker beginning a microdosing journey, I have a personal affinity for mushrooms and will reference them throughout this work. But other things like LSD or mescaline work just fine as well, so please do not take me to mean that I think *only* mushrooms present viable gateways for microdosing magic—far from it!

Just a preference for me. ☺

Alchemy, a magical precursor to chemical engineering, once flourished in the medieval European university. Alchemists believed in a natural and spiritual hierarchy that pervaded the entire universe. Each natural object, whether mineral, vegetable, animal, or human was subject to the "dominion" of its immediate superior. So, for example, plants were subject to insects that were subject to small animals that were subject to large animals that were subject to humans.

Broken down even further we see early whispers of evolution in the alchemical arts as well, centuries before Darwinism. The rationale went in this wise: all metals went through an evolutionary process, starting as lead, evolving into bronze, then copper, then silver, then finally, gold. For this principle alchemists would famously attempt to turn lead into gold, endeavoring to speed up this process by a variety of strenuous and intricate methods that included astrology, crude chemistry, and herbalism.

This concept was not lost on the alchemist herself. Indeed, part of alchemical exercise included trying to find an "elixir of immortality," a potion that, once drunk, would evolve the alchemist into a higher, divine, state of being. In some less than romantic episodes, medieval and Renaissance alchemists would drink liquefied gold to achieve this higher state of awareness.

Their family and friends missed them dearly ….

Thankfully, we today have a far healthier (and infinitely less dangerous) food of immortality allied with us. Might we have found the elixir of immortality in the magic mushroom?

In the ancient pagan world, *wisdom* was often represented by serpents (this rule infamously inverted as "shrewdness" in the Garden of Eden story). So much so, that magical women were sometimes referred to as "pythia priestesses," and small statuettes often depict them holding serpents, which symbolized psychedelic and medicinal plants and fungi.

Thousands of years later, modern clinical trials and personal testimonials are confirming what the ancients already knew: mushrooms are not only medicinal, but also show promise for neurogenesis. We today can look at those little psilocybin entities peering through the soil or dung as serpents rising from the Earth.

Happily some of the other neurogenesis-stimulating mushroom culprits here, the lion's mane and reishi, are totally legal and can be found at your local health food store or online fungus supplier. A number of clinical studies beginning in the early 1990s have demonstrated this remarkable alchemical secret of the lion's mane. More recently, in 2009, scientists tested lion's mane on a group of 15 people aged 50 – 80 against a control group (of equal size) given placebos. Each group received their doses for 16 weeks, taking cognitive tests at weeks 8, 12, and 16. Those in the experimental group outscored the control group each time during the 16 week period.

The doctors followed the 16 week session with

four weeks of observation and testing. Surprisingly, by the fourth week, the experimental group's scores had diminished noticeably. The study drew two conclusions: first, that lion's mane mushrooms appeared to stimulate cognitive function; and second, that the tests "showed no adverse effect" from eating the mushroom.[1]

Myelin and mycelium

The secret of the lion's mane has to do with its ability to regenerate myelin ("remyelination") in the central nervous system. Myelin is a fatty sleeve that sheathes nerve cells. This noble covering reinforces the nerve channels so that the tiny explosions that carpet-bomb our central nervous system every second of our lives are directed correctly and end up at the proper destination. Science writer Courtney Sperlazza compares the relationship of nerve to myelin with insulated wires. Open wires will shock anything they touch, while the colorful plastic wraps keep the electricity contained and flowing along the circuit.[2]

Myelin is good shit. It provides numerous benefits to the human experience, including mood enhancement, problem solving, sensory perception, memory, and overall IQ. Similar effects have even been observed in rats fed the mushrooms; these furry little critters also showed something else quite remarkable: signs of curiosity![3]

1. Mori et. al., "Improving effects of the mushroom Yamabushitake ...," in *Phytotherapy Research*, March 2009;23(3), pgs. 367-72.
2. Courtney Sperlazza," What You Need to Know About Myelin ...," Bulletproof Blog; accessed via: blog.bulletproof.com.
3. Mori, K., et. al. (2011) Effects of Hericium erinaceus on amyloid β (25-35) ... in mice," in *Biomedical Research* 2009, 32(1), pgs. 67-72.

Even if you have no interest in microdosing psilocybin mushrooms, eating lion's mane mushrooms daily is still a legal way to improve your mood and boost your creativity. Currently, no clinical studies exist outlining the effects of mixing lion's mane and psilocybin. Though, it should also be said that both mushrooms are totally physiologically safe by themselves.

Beats drinking liquid gold.

Another "over the counter" medicinal mushroom is the so-called "mushroom of immortality," the reishi mushroom, which has been used for centuries in Chinese medicine. Aside from numerous health risks that the mushroom guards against like diabetes, liver problems, and high blood pressure, the reishi also battles fatigue, insomnia, and depression.

Like the promises of the lion's mane mushroom, the reishi mushroom has not been tested alongside psilocybin mushrooms in clinical studies to determine their possible mutual efficacy. But in the very least these conversations are happening now in ways that they were not happening only 50 years ago.

△

As for procuring the psilocybin mushrooms to eat beside the lion's mane and reishi, well, the true beauty of the mushroom is simple: they grow *everywhere*. If you are on the western coasts, drive to grassy beach areas and find azurescens. On a farm? Start digging through cow shit for cubensis; live near grasslands and meadows? Psilocybin semilanceata (Liberty Caps) might be growing nearby.[4] An excellent online resource, mushroomobserver.org, has informative materials on different kinds of mushrooms, where they grow, and what times of year they sprout. However, one should never pick wild mushrooms with imprudence. A psychedelic mushroom will grow side by side with a mushroom that will kill you.

The best ways to prepare are:

1. Get yourself a good field guide. Paul Stamets' *Psilocybin Mushrooms of the World* is still the go-to for any serious mushroom hunter.

2. Find a guide who knows her mycology or take a class on wild mushroom collecting.

3. Join a mycology club. You can check the national directory at www.namyco.org.

4. Do all three.

Mushrooms are very powerful teachers and allies that can be found, harvested, dried, and eaten without any middle-person involved whatsoever—from Gaia's teat to your Soul.

Just be careful!

---

4. What makes the Liberty Cap so desirable is that it usually contains about the same amount of psilocybin across the globe, making gauging doses easy. See Andy Letcher, *Shroom: A Cultural History of the Magic Mushroom* (Harper Perennial, 2008), p.168.

DOSE SIZES

Now that we have a relationship with our fungal allies, let's get into the magic of proper dosing! There are at least four kinds of doses of which I am aware. While I utilize all four for my practices and purposes, and will give a brief outline of each here, I designed the spells in this book with only microdosing and threshold dosing in mind.

MICRODOSE (VITAMIN DOSE) (0.2 – 0.4 grams)

I tend to refer to "microdosing" as "vitamin" dosing for the following reason: firstly, many people ask me how much (in milligrams) a microdose weighs. A microdose usually ranges between 0.2 – 0.4 grams. But since we are each our own cosmic chemistry lab, I would also like to give a universal answer that also addresses why I refer to microdosing as "vitamin" dosing. A microdose should be so small that you don't feel it; like a vitamin. Consider this: when you were younger and took Flintstone Vitamins did you ever feel like you were high on Betty Rubble? Of course not. Such is the point of the microdose.

How big should the dose be?

Vitamin sized![5]

Microdosing has become quite the vogue in recent years, although the phenomenon has been erroneously credited to Silicon Valley. There are in fact predecessors. For me, microdosing started way back in the late 90s when

5. Since the term "microdosing" has become so embedded in our popular culture I will stick with that term throughout this work.

my buddies and I could only afford one eighth or so of mushrooms between us. In those days, we didn't call it "microdosing" or "vitamin dosing"; we called it "being broke." Still, we certainly weren't the first ones to stumble upon the benefits of microdosing. Buddhist scholar (and dashing gentleman) Mike Crowley has pointed out that a vow taken as part of the Nying-Tik Yab-Shi initiation into the Longchen Nying-Tik ("Longchenpa's Heart Essence") tradition of Dzogchen included eating amrita in small amounts daily for the subdued, beneficial physical effects. And perhaps those Egyptian priests who ate mushrooms and hemlock so as to sit still in the temple all day took them in wee-small amounts?[6]

THRESHOLD DOSE (roughly 0.6 – 0.9 grams)

This particular dose doesn't have a fixed name, although I have recently heard it referred to as a "minidose."[7] The threshold dose differs from the microdose in that with the former you feel the effects of the mushrooms (but not intensely). With threshold dosing you are in two realities: waking reality and pixie reality. I will not lie to you, dear seeker, the threshold space can feel very uncomfortable. It is like standing in a doorway, a threshold that allows you to keep one foot in this space and the other foot in the magical space. Here, you are literally "entranced": standing

6. Remondino in Wooster, *Pacific Medical Journal*, pg. 527.
7. Paul Austin (2017), unpaged. Since "minidose" isn't as embedded in popular terminology as "microdose," I will continue with the term "threshold dose."

in the doorway of magic. But it is also a perfect space for challenging oneself to do simple tasks more creatively (see chapter 9). I like to take a threshold dose on a free day wherein I do menial tasks around the house and yard.

PSYCHEDELIC DOSE (1.5 – 3.5 grams)

A psychedelic dose is essentially a magical dose. I save my magical dosing for special occasions when I want to do some deep spiritual work. Both feet are firmly in the magical realm. This is the place where phenomena happen.

HERO DOSE (5+ grams)

When Terence McKenna first coined the term "hero dose" he was referring to eating five grams of mushrooms, lying down on a bed or couch, closing his eyes, and drifting away into eternity. I think a hero dose can be done with any psychedelic. For, like all psychedelic magic, it is the state of awareness that matters more than the substance used to get there. The hero dose allows for a most beneficial endeavor: complete surrender.

> In life, we need to learn how to let go.
> The hero dose accomplishes that kind of magic.

.3.

Symbol Cycles to Rune Your Day
Setting a Microdose Schedule

Different experts have different advice outlining their preferred way to microdose. Renowned mycologist Paul Stamets recommends taking a dose Monday through Friday, abstaining Saturday and Sunday. James Fadiman (PhD), however, thinks a few days "on" a few days "off" is sufficient. In a way, both are correct. We really don't know much about the long-term effects of microdosing yet; but, given the lengthy history of eating these magical fruits, there is nothing to suggest future deleteriousness.

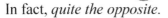

In fact, *quite the opposite.*

I have found that tying my microdosing intention to a simple symbol has had a noticeable impact. Symbols are recognizable to us the moment we see them. Symbols range from those that the majority of us can easily identify (a crucifix, the Golden Arches, etc.) to ones closer to home (a family crest) to even personal symbols of joy and empowerment detectable only to you (a lucky bracelet). They stir Emotion and Intellect, serving as magical reminders; the domain of the symbol is in the past and present—some association we have made with the symbol in the past affects us in the present. Symbols work within the conscious mind.

Symbols provide an easy way for beginners to set a microdosing cycle without overdoing it. You can use existing symbols (see the following page) or create your own using a dose cycle symbol graph. To make a simple symbol cycle, first draw a box. Add six horizontal lines and a series of vertical lines (as many as needed) across the box so that it looks like graph paper. Put the days of the week above each of the seven columns. The horizontal columns represent weeks, beginning with Week 1 at the top.

Now decide on a symbol and "dot" it out in the smaller boxes of the cycle graph. I'll demonstrate this with an easy symbol: the pentacle. When placed on a symbol chart, the pentacle microdose cycle looks like this (plate 3.1). It provides an easy and safe way to start microdosing.

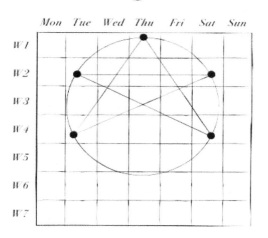

(3.1)

This cycle takes four weeks:

Week One: Microdose on Thursday.
Week Two: Microdose on Tuesday and Saturday.
Week Three: No microdose.
Week Four: Microdose on Tuesday and Saturday.

Bright side of the rune

Runes ("letters") provide another magically fun way to
set a magical intention beyond just keeping a dose cycle.
Runes are rooted in old Germanic lore, holding occult
powers. For Germanic runes have two meanings: the sound
of the requisite letter and a symbolic association. So, for
example, the rune "R" both symbolizes and retains the
letter "r" and also signifies the word *rad* or "journey."[1]

1. Gale R. Owens, *Rites and Religions of the Anglo- Saxons*, pg. 55.

Readers of Jewish mysticism might recognize a hint of *abracadabra* ("and that which was spoken was made manifest") buried in Germanic rune magic.

For our purposes we will use these runes as an easy way to run a dose cycle with magical intention. The most general of the runes (that do not deal with gods) number five themes:

1. Wealth (*feoh*): As one might expect, the word originally meant "livestock," but over time has been regarded as any material capital.

2. Cooperative joy (*wyn*): This word most nearly means "enjoyment of a stable position," usually relating to a work setting (i.e., relations with bosses and coworkers). This is a great rune dose cycle to run if you are just starting a new job or want to improve the atmosphere at a current one. Interestingly, anecdotal evidence has already shown microdosing to improve this. James Fadiman once quipped how microdosing allows a person to "find the office jerk bearable … you're more compassionate about the flaws of others."[2]

3. Generosity (*gyfu*): Tis true—giving is awesome! The receiver feels great, you feel great—win, win! This is a good schedule to run if you have a surprise party you are planning for someone or even just

---

2. Olivia Solon, "Meet the Silicon Valley-ites taking tiny hits of LSD to boost performance," *Wired* (24, August, 16); accessed via: wired.co.uk.

want to think creatively about how to give more to your loved ones. It is also just a great cycle for which to reflect upon basic gratitude.

4. Rebirth (*beorc*): *Beorc* translates to "birch tree," a symbol of fertility (and therefore rebirth) in medieval Europe (specifically the Germanic areas).

5. Journey (*rad*): We today derive our word "ride" from *rad*. Indeed, in our modern world of easy travel via plane, train, and automobile, travel is as easy and safe as ever. The word may also hold some spiritual underpinnings as well. Are not psychedelic and heroic doses "trips," at least according to common parlance? This is a good cycle to run leading up to a psychedelic or hero dose.

6. Achievement (*ur*): This rune symbolizes the wild ox and may point to an ancient Germanic rite: young men would have to wrestle and fell an ox to confirm their strength and manhood. The rune came to symbolize all forms of triumph.

△

Of course if you already have a symbol that tickles your fancy (one you came across elsewhere or one you've designed yourself) those can hold equal power. Should you desire to begin with one of the runes mentioned above, the cycles look like these:

WEALTH

	Mon	Tue	Wed	Thu	Fri	Sat	Sun
W1	●			●			
W2	●		●				
W3	●	●	●				
W4	●	●					
W5	●						
W6	●						
W7	●						

COOPERATIVE JOY

	Mon	Tue	Wed	Thu	Fri	Sat	Sun
W1	●						
W2	●	●					
W3	●		●				
W4	●	●					
W5	●						
W6	●						
W7	●						

GENEROSITY

	Mon	Tue	Wed	Thu	Fri	Sat	Sun
W1	●						●
W2		●				●	
W3			●		●		
W4				●			
W5			●		●		
W6		●				●	
W7	●						●

REBIRTH

	Mon	Tue	Wed	Thu	Fri	Sat	Sun
W1	●						
W2	●	●					
W3	●		●				
W4	●	●					
W5	●		●				
W6	●	●					
W7	●						

Journey

	Mon	Tue	Wed	Thu	Fri	Sat	Sun
W1	●						
W2	●	●					
W3	●		●				
W4	●	●					
W5	●		●				
W6	●			●			
W7	●				●		

Achievement

	Mon	Tue	Wed	Thu	Fri	Sat	Sun
W1	●	●	●				
W2	●			●			
W3	●				●		
W4	●				●		
W5	●				●		
W6	●				●		
W7	●				●		

.4.

SIDE EFFECTS OF MICRODOSING

A PURGE(ATORY) STORY

So here's a weird one.

Aside from the usual claims coming from people who microdose (i.e., focus, retention, productivity, kicking ass, overall improvement in mental, emotional, and spiritual wellbeing) there has been little to no talk about some of the more physiological effects of running a dose cycle. But I noticed something about my microdosing experiences that (while a little embarrassing) has also led me to some discoveries that I have found useful enough to share here.

T[...]r innocuous (though, at times, very inconveni[...] physiological discharges that I have found can [...] ny microdose cycles include: yawning, frequent ur[...] pontaneous crying, and relentless horniness.

Wei[...]

I will [...] s so much on the first two as I am neither an uro[...] r a yawnician. They are just minor physiological [...] ns that I have noted in my magical journal. They [...] d go (say, on a 10 - 30 day cycle, I might experien[...] extra urination and yawning 3 – 4 days during the s[...] ting). Often they appear on the first few days and even[...] disappear. A friend of mine sees both as signs of bod[...] urging of latent toxins—the kind of shit people get colonics to remedy.

As for the latter two, spontaneous crying and horniness ... well, even after half a lifetime studying exotic, lost cultures in history, remains the oddest pairing of concepts I have ever written. The horniness most likely arises as a natural extension of the slight euphoric feelings (the "body high") of the micro/threshold dose. And while I haven't seen it addressed much since the microdose movement,[1] it has turned up in history with regards to higher doses. Franciscan monk Bernardino de Sahagún (c. 1500 – 1590), an ethnographer who spent twenty years traveling throughout Mexico learning the Aztec language, noted in his *Florentine Codex* (1590) that those

---

1. A notable exception appears in Ben Sessa, *The Psychedelic Renaissance*, p. 80.

most magical mushrooms eaten by the locals "provoke[d] lust."[2] In more recent decades (the late 1950s) Eunice Pike and Florence Cowan, two Bible translators attempting to eradicate a highly Christianized mushroom religion from the Mazatec of Oaxaca, Mexico, observed a certain "taboo" among the locals. Before participation in a mushroom ceremony, they abstained from sex for four or five days before and after the ritual. In fact, the Mazatec had *so* wed the mushroom to the Scriptures that they often gave up both (shroom and scripture) once married![3] Pioneering mushroom researcher John W. Allen believes this has to do with the extreme pleasure gained from experiencing intercourse while "talking to God" through the mushroom. Such over-stimulation and pleasure would drive a person crazy. While I feel that Allen has misread the situation,[4] many mushroom-eaters have told him that adding intercourse to mushrooms equaled "the finest madness they have ever experienced."[5]

But the reviews are mixed, as summed up by one poster, Akari, on the psychedelic message board, *mycotopia.net*: "Everytime [*sic*] I do mushrooms with my

2. Quoted in Reay Tannahill, *Food in History* (UK: Eyre Methuen, 1973), pg. 259.
3 . Eunice Pike and Florence Cowan, "Mushroom Ritual verses Christianity" in *Practical Anthropology*, Vol. 6, No. 4 (July-August 1959), pp. 145-150.
4. The Mazatec seem to abstain from many things considered "unclean" during the mushroom ceremony; see Eunice V. Pike, "Mazatec Sexual Impurity and Bible Reading," in *Practical Anthropology*, Volume 7 (2): 49-53.
5. John W. Allen, "Effects of psilocybin," *Mycotopia Web Archive*, 23, August, 01. He has collected a wealth of testimonials regarding the use of mushrooms over his lifetime.

wife, she get's [sic] all horny. I get all holy though. ... all I can think about is totally insane shit, like am I really God? Is there a God? Is there a heaven and hell? Or shit like that ... And she's upset ..."[6]

This gentleman (indeed all of the above examples as well) is referring to higher doses of mushrooms, those in the psychedelic dose range. Personally, I have never tried to have sex on a high dose of mushrooms; sounds ... scary. And anyway, the horniness I experience while micro- and threshold dosing is something quite different from having sex while on mushrooms in that the horniness from the former does not just occur during the dose itself, but pervades the enter cycle (and a week or so after). During that time I bathe and robe myself with all the enjoyment and fervor of a proper epicurean! It's even more stimulating (for obvious reasons) during late April through early June, when our sun is gifting us its rich and luxurious Persephone vitamins.

If you find your libido is no more or less excited than normal during a dose cycle feel free to skip ahead. However, if you are finding that mushrooms stir your carnal instincts perhaps try the following sex magic mushroom spell to release it. Your kinks and shadow side are more powerful than you think.

The reason sex has so much influence in magic has to do with the creative phenomena invoked by such ancient ecstatic energy. The waves that pour through our body

6. "They Get Horny and Holy at the Same Time," 5, August, 11; accessed via: mycotopia.net.

in such a state can be focused outwardly into the world, carrying magical intentions into the Realm of Possibility.

These same magical waves can also be produced with deep, concentrated meditation, and psilocybin mushrooms (our spell will employ all three). When you send that energy into the space around you the shifts you are trying to create come even more into your attention.

So if you are feeling extra plucky …

Ascension spell

This spell requires getting in touch with your deepest sexual gratifications in a fun manner either with your partner(s) or, given the unfortunate stigma that surrounds exotic sexual habits, in the company of your preferred hand.

Since this kind of spell should be done while in the process of your dose cycle there is no appointed day to harvest the erotic discharges. Still, some consideration must be paid to the day, as you need to farm your juices *before* a day of significance to you (your birthday, New Year's Eve, the day you quit smoking cigarettes, etc.). The day I chose was New Year's Eve, 2017. Coincidentally, I had been on a dose cycle anyway (engaged in creativity magic finishing my book *Psychedelic Mystery Traditions*), so my biological instincts had already been revved through the mushrooms. I decided to hold off and not hold on to my little fellow for a few days. I bid my dear lover adieu for about a week and *saved* that burst.

41

On Thursday, 21 December 2017, the Winter Solstice, I made a sigil (see chapter 7) that expressed my desire to grow, learn, and be more compassionate in 2018. I put myself in a deep waking dream state through a suffumigation of cannabis, mandrake, and henbane. These latter two plants are known as the "hexing herbs" of medieval witchcraft—and damn, do they live up to that name! The state of mind caused by mixing the three herbs can be fantastically unpleasant without deep practice with them. Since most people do not work with the hexing herbs (I don't recommend it), feel free to use the medicines of your choice during the extraction process.

Once in that enchanted state, I did my usual meditation→visualization and let my basest fantasies run amok, feverishly making sure that one part of my body was shinier than the rest. Just as I was about to erupt, I did my best to visualize the sigil in my head. Difficult as it was, I managed to get a clear picture of it in my mind's-eye for a few seconds as I reaped the essential juice, which was collected in a tissue. I put the tissue and the sigil in the small cauldron that sits at the center of the pentacle on my altar.

There it sat until New Year's Eve. I had a small gathering of magical friends over that evening (otherwise known 'round these parts as a "Love Party") to add as much energy as I could to the spell. All who came knew my intention and were on-board for the rite. Those who were not left before midnight. I went around and asked each of my friends in what way they wished to contribute in a positive way to 2018. At one point we were all in my room dancing, chanting, passing joints, and inhaling a variety of burning hexing herbs. When the energy built to an ecstatic fervor a few minutes before midnight, I finally lit the contents of the small cauldron so that it would burn from 2017 and carry the charged Solstice juice and accompanying sigil flames into 2018. I asked my friends to think about their promise for positive growth in the New Year. At midnight I took some ashes from the horrors of Mount Vesuvius[7] and sprinkled them over the burning remains in the cauldron saying, "We have all charged this spell with our personal intentions for positive change this year. We will live this positive change, lest we perish covered in the ashes of Vesuvius."

STEPS

1. Decide on a date of significance for you, whether personal or public.

2. Create a sigil around your desire.

3. A week or so before that date, take a dose of whatever you prefer and meditate→visualize on your basest fantasies. The baser the better!

4. Collect magical juices and sigil into any fire-safe container (metal chalice, cauldron, skull of your

---

7. A friend gifted me some after she returned from a visit to Pompeii.

former enemy, etc.).

5. On appointed night, burn the contents in whatever way you see fit at midnight (inviting magical friends over is a great excuse to get the gang together!).

6. Let the fumes carry your desires into the coming years.

This spell ended up having some very interesting results (see chapter 10). Anyway, that's the kind of stuff you can do if you find that microdosing is stirring the erotic fires in your belly!

▽

Still with me?

Good, because I was most surprised by the following discharge.

Crying. I started to cry. A lot. Sometimes for no reason whatsoever, other than a song triggering a memory. Of course music can seduce our Emotion but—and I can only speak for myself—not until I started microdosing did such song-triggered memories result in physical tears.

Needless to say, it started to get inconvenient …

A ridiculous example (but it'll underscore my point) had to do with paying my taxes. I do not mean to say I started to cry because paying taxes sucks. Quite the opposite! I was happy because I hadn't had a steady income or any money for years. Finally in a position where I could pay taxes I started crying tears of joy! And I did it right in front of my tax agent on the day I met her! I dunno, we just had a really good connection. I was just so … so *grateful*. I doubt I would have had such a reAction had I not been on a microdose cycle. This embarrassing little run-in served as a *strong* reminder for me that our mind creates our brain (i.e., "what's the mind?").

I think that sometimes we just need a good cry. Consider all the negative information that batters us daily—war, famine, disease, civil rights abuses. And it's not as if we are actively suppressing or ignoring all the bad news. We are all just too busy trying to get by to do anything more than take notice, be upset for a moment, argue on social media, forget, and move on with our lives.

But I do not think we *really* forget. I think these things collect in our subconscious minds, building up as psychic garbage that slowly overtime gum up our works. Then one day we are just kinda pissed off … *and we don't even know why.*

Like the mushrooms, our puppies and kitties are very in touch with our Emotion, even when we aren't. One of the greatest gifts our little furry companions give us is support during times that test Emotion. Therefore this microdose spell can be used to test your level of Emotional buildup. If you have dealt with your Emotion in healthy ways previously, this may have little effect on you. As

45

for me, I decided that I needed to channel whatever those Emotional blockages were into a spell.

The Withes' Kitty is just such a spell! I use it to purge pent up negative Emotion during dose cycles in a safe, supportive environment. There is no appointed day to try this spell. But if you feel that microdosing is having a similar effect on your eyes at inopportune moments, consider trying the following:

THE WITCHES' KITTY (BUT PUPPIES ARE COOL TOO!)

Grab your favorite kitty or two (puppies are cool too[8]). Sit with your little companion(s) and go to youtube.com.

Type in "Christian the Lion."

…………..

Let it out.

Go on … *let it out.*

Let it out and remember.

Remember that there is love and friendship. There is love even recognized by the most unlikely creatures! And don'tchajus love those insufferably adorable videos of ducks that befriend pigs, elephants that marry dogs, and a host of other magical animal friends that find each other?! Beyond the barrage of bad news hammered upon us by a manipulative media, there is love, friendship, and cuteness—all things that satisfy healthy Emotion!

---

8. As a helpless cat person, I will move forward with kitty pronouns for ease.

Counterbalance that built-up psychic garbage deep within Emotion with the *truth* that love is more powerful than hate. Even the love of those lost—for we are reflections of the lessons they instilled in our hearts. Your kitty will be there to protect you. Purring her little heart out against your chest and absorbing, and then recycling, that Emotional psychic trash build-up into tears of joy, companionship, and love.

Kitty magic!

You are never alone.

Those purrs guarantee it.

△

Once I did this ritual the spontaneous crying ceased.

I was free!

If one is up for this kind of deep Emotional magic, one need not stay with "Christian the Lion." That video just so happens to work for me. Watch/listen to/read whatever video, song, or poem works for you.

So put your guard down.

Get that Emotion in right relation with your Intellect and Will.

And let it out.

Breathe.

Kitty. Magic.

.5.

MICRODOSE SPELLS TO UN-ASSHOLE YOURSELF
BECAUSE THE WORLD NEEDS YOU NOW MORE THAN EVER!

One of the benefits I like the most from microdosing is that it widens the gap between action and reAction, allowing me to think more clearly before saying or doing something that I would, in all likelihood, later regret.

One day on a mountain I took a psychedelic dose of mushrooms with my partner Eden. Among dozens of other thoughts that flooded my mind that day, a single idea kept cycling back to some kind of philosophical starting point like a series of landings ascending the staircase of life. Only this time I was able to expand the space between action and reAction and scrutinize the interior. There sat a single thought that I had never really unpacked before: "Tom, you are a good fellow, *but you can be a real asshole sometimes.*" Sure. We all know that; such an assessment could easily apply to, well, nearly all of us. But I realized something about it that I never thought before, which spawned a question: just how much of the "good fellow" is negated by the "asshole?" For some people who I have been especially assholic towards, probably all of it!

This will not do.

The problem is that assholery is an inadvertent purge caused by backed-up Emotion and Intellect bullshit and stress. So if you skipped The Witches' Kitty please consider giving it a go.

Otherwise, there is one thing each of us can do. It is political, apolitical, theological, secular, collective, and individual all at once. It is something that we ought to consider every time we ask ourselves "how did things get this way?" The thing that we can all do, whether we veer to the political left, right, or something in the middle, is remove one asshole from the planet. That's it. How do you remove one asshole from the planet? Simple: you don't be an asshole.

A great way to do that is to cast ego-tempering spells to un-asshole yourself.

EGO TEMPERING SPELLS

Many in the psychedelic Renaissance refer to "ego

death"—that moment when, under the influence of a psychedelic, all ego vanishes and the explorer of inner-space losses all sense of self. It's definitely a good time! However, while this ego death is only temporary, some make the error of believing that their ego has been permanently annihilated. A hypothetical statement from this kind of person usually sounds something like this: "*I* killed *my* ego and *you* need to listen to *me* about how *I* did it! Can't *you* see how much more *I* know about ego-death than do *you*?!"

Clearly, the ego is still fully intact.

But I understand the philosophy. Ego can get in the way of some very important lessons in life. Ego can cloud judgment, ruin relationships, and if kept unchecked has the ability to bring unnecessary grief to a person's life. Still it is what makes you who you are and it is necessary to get along in this plane of existence. And anyway, I like you! If your ego died, I'd miss you. ☹ Since we are born natural egoists and therefore can never truly escape it any more than we can escape breathing air, I prefer not striving for ego *death*, but rather ego *tempering*.

Ego tempering is yoga for arrogance, ensuring we stay aligned in the universe, not sectioned off in the "youniverse." For while it is possible to achieve great things through the ego alone, such an avenue will limit your ability to work with others and critique yourself. Therefore, egos are the only thing that should be exercised in reverse. Or rather, you shouldn't *exercise* your ego, you should *exorcize* it. Microdosing and ego-tempering spells serve such a purpose.

And here's how I do it!

First, I set up a magical dose schedule that represents the elimination of my inner-asshole via tempering of the ego. An upside-down "A" (see plate 5.1) is a good, general symbol of intention. It is the reverse of *A*sshole; (but, of course, set up your cycle as you wish.)

	Mon	Tue	Wed	Thu	Fri	Sat	Sun
W1	●						●
W2	●						●
W3	●						●
W4	●		●	●	●		●
W5		●				●	
W6			●		●		
W7				●			

(5.1)

I prefer the upside-down "A" because I am instantly reminded of my intention every day of the dose cycle that I am under a spell and cannot be an asshole. The schedule alone holds that kind of magic.☺

On each of the sixteen days that I take my microdose for this cycle I temper my ego in one of the following ways:

51

1. On some days of the cycle I do not use the term "I" at all. It both forces me to come up with new, creative ways to say sentences during conversations while combating the very real, creeping (and crippling) solipsism that is all too difficult to avoid in the age of social media.

2. I "lose my voice" for a day (a day off from work is preferable). I go about my usual interactions, but do not say a word for 24 hours. I have to rely on only meaningful gestures, universal hand signals, eye contact, and body language to communicate.

3. Handwrite a complimentary letter to someone who has wronged me. It's interesting to consider how that person has affected me in positive ways and let her, him, or they know in the letter. This is not a "forgiveness" letter; it is a "thank you" letter. This letter is never sent. But it helps grudges, and therefore ego, fade.

4. Simply meditate on the fact that nobody owes me anything and it is a gift to be here.

5. Stay off social media for the entire cycle. (This is actually choice advice for all magical microdose cycles).

6. Remember: everyone lacks some piece of information that the majority of us consider "common knowledge." Be nice when that happens.

7. Take a break from a habit (smoking, watching too much TV/Internet, etc.) and stay focused on the *fact* that you are

currently under a spell and not allowed to let those itches manifest in assholery towards the people you love.

8. If owed, give someone a *real* apology. Not the lawyer-scripted bullshit kind.

9. If someone gives a gift, pay more attention to that person's joy of giving than to your pleasure of receiving. Feel the *giver's* pleasure, not your own (this is a Kabbalistic concept that we will further explore in the next chapter).

10. If you meet someone new during the cycle do not adhere to the belief that a person only gets "one first impression." I disagree. I've met people that have been downright mean and spiteful only to find out that I happened to meet that person on one of the worst days of her, their, or his life. We all have bad days. So when I meet someone for the first time, I never really allow them to make an impression on me—even if it's positive. Indeed, the opposite could be true: I could have met a really funny and happy guy on a day when he just cheated someone in some way. Maybe that's why he is in such a good mood? I never know.

Best not let my ego assume.

△

Anyway, these are just some of the things I do to temper my ego during this particular spellcasting cycle (and whenever needed). Of the many ways one can expand one's mind, simply knowing and admitting when one is wrong is among the best. ☺ I find that these exercises help me through *prevention* rather than *cure* by stretching the space between action and reAction. On each day of this deassholèfication cycle, if you feel like you are growing impatient, close your eyes, center yourself, and say the word "love."

It's fine to have an ego.

Just don't let it rule you.

Otherwise you shield your eyes from the universal perspective, which is our collected human wisdom as gifted from the cosmos. It is far easier to take positive Action if your Intellect is balanced with your Emotion and Will.

HOW TO LIVE FOREVER: A CHANCE MEETING WITH MR. D.

While on my way to Las Vegas for RollerCon[1] I stopped over in St. Louis, Missouri, to play five roller derby bouts in two days with the New York Shock Exchange against the St. Louis GateKeepers. As I waited at the bus stop to make my way to Lambert Airport, an elderly gentleman came walking up to wait for the bus as well. He asked me for the time.

"[Whatever] o' clock," I replied.

I enjoy talking to strangers (especially my elders – they always have the best stories!) so I struck up a conversation with this man who identified himself only as

1. A five day party for derbyfolk.

54

Mr. D. He asked me where I was headed and I (of course) used that as an excuse to pontificate about roller derby.

But, so as not to be rude, I interrupted myself and asked him where he was headed. He said that he was on his way to meet his brother so as to celebrate the latter's 93rd birthday!

When I responded that his brother's age was most impressive Mr. D informed me that he was, in fact, 96 years old himself! More stunningly, Mr. D used my shock to inform me that his father had lived to be 112!

We continued to talk about this and that until the conversation came to a natural termination. A few moments went by and I finally decided to ask: "Mr. D, if you do not mind my asking … you said that your brother turns 93 today, you are 96, and your father lived to be 112. I gotta ask ... what's the secret to longevity?"

Mr. D furrowed his brow – shocked by such an ignorant question. "Longevity?" he replied. "That's easy. There are 24 hours in a day. For the first 12 hours take care of your own business. During the other 12 hours stay out of other peoples' business. Do that and you'll live to be 112, just like muh daddy."

How about you? Do you find yourself talking more about other peoples' drama than about shaping your own creations? Perhaps one of the most beneficial ego-tempering spells to cast on oneself is to not waste your Four Gifts muddying up the lives of others. Instead, use your magic to align the Four Gifts and create a better world for yourself; this inevitably trickles out to those around you.

The next time you feel you are butting into someone else's business—especially during an ego-tempering, Intellect-satisfying, microdose cycle—remember you are under a spell and must ignore it.

Death can wait.

▽

To close our section on spells that deassholèfy ourselves, I would like to share a story that I think best exemplifies the end result that microdosing and the above spells had on soothing my ego. It was the time that the gap between action and reAction due to microdosing ego-tempering spells was most prominent.

It had been snowing and sleeting and raining and snowing and raining and sleeting as the gods poured divine diarrhea upon us mortals, making even going to the mailbox unbearable.

Unable to stay cooped up any longer I decided to bundle up, borrow my roommate's large umbrella, and go for a walk in the slushy, snowy rain. Cars appeared few and far between—no surprise considering the unsafe condition of the roads. At a stoplight not far from my house a guy driving a small pickup decided he was going to veer his wheel into a patch of icy water and splash me. He succeeded.

But he also lost control of his car and skidded off the road, slightly t-boning a pole and dinging a parked car.

"That's what you get for fucking with a witch!" I yelled. I was drenched and went home to change before confronting him. I couldn't wait to rub it in his face.

But then something happened as I put large plastic bags over my new, dry socks to slide my feet into my still-wet sneakers: I had a change of Intellect. A subtle epiphany from the mushrooms told me to resist the desire for revenge. To not let Emotion control me. In our culture today we are, in my opinion, all getting a little too eager to ruin someone's life over the smallest transgression. It's as if we are cheapening real victimhood with love of the spotlight when we get to tell everyone, "Yes! I have been wronged! I, too, deal with shit! Cater to me!"

But according to my mushroom teachers and the ego-tempering spellwork that accompanied their lessons, it was time to break that cycle of vengeance and grudges, if only in myself. It was time to break the cycle of ego. It was time to un-asshole myself. This guy's thoughts and opinions about me—well ... *they were none of my damn business!*

By the time I walked the 75 or so feet from my front door to the scene a few people had gathered. I told the owner of the parked car that I was a witness to the incident. He asked about the driver and I told him that the guy was driving as safely as anyone would (considering the condition of the roads).

The driver was in shock.

When all was said and done (there was no real

damage but a few scrapes on both cars that the owners decided to just settle without paperwork, insurance companies, and bullshit), the driver took me aside and asked me why I didn't turn him in.

The truth is I was fine physically; it was my *ego* that felt bruised from the splashing. But then, admittedly, only in the moment. Is a momentarily bruised ego really worth potentially ruining this guy's life (perhaps he had a driving job of some kind and would be fired if reported)? What if he had a family? Kids? There was far more at play than my temporarily bruised ego.

I didn't say all that, settling on something closer to:

"I don't think you are really a bad person. The weather has been frustrating for everyone and we are all feeling the effects from it."

He reached for his wallet like he wanted to pay me off.

"I don't want your money," I said.

"How can I repay you?" he asked.

"Just remember," I replied.

It took a moment, but he eventually understood.

"Okay. … I will," he said.

We shook hands and I continued my walk through the sleet and snow and hail and diarrhea that the gods shat upon us. With a bit of luck, *two* former assholes walked away from the scene.

Most everyone means something to someone. And we all have to get along. The person whose life you may be eager to ruin over some minor transgressions on one day is the same person who, on a different day, would tend to you in a moment of need. Let's expand the space between action and reAction with some microdosing, ego-tempering spells, and wise words from Mr. D.

And live forever. ☺

.6.

PENTACLES, KABBALAH, AND MICRODOSING
HOW TO ALIGN THE LAW

In the previous chapter I had touched briefly upon the Kabbalistic concept of receiving pleasure through another's joy. Let's incorporate some more rudimentary Kabbalistic concepts and work in some microdosing techniques. Kabbalists usually work with a system known as the Tree of Life. Mastery of the Tree of Life has been said to grant a perspective that leads to wisdom in the face of any challenge; the byproduct of which results in contentment in this life. Understanding the paths and circuitry of the Tree takes years of practice and discipline that is beyond the scope of this little spellbook. Therefore, I will forego its discussion despite the essential nature of it within the Kabbalistic discipline.

On the other paw, another principle called the Kabbalistic Law seems reasonable enough with which to dissect and work. The Law goes in this wise: since we are born conscious egoists (immaterial) and only recognize the mutual benefits of give and take through society (material), it is a natural extension of the Law that we should enjoy all the benefits of society so long as we contribute to it. Literally, *everything* you enjoy was created by the mutual cooperation of natural products (material, Action) with society (immaterial, the Three Spiritual Forces).

In today's hectic (and often tragic) world it can be easy to overlook or forget this Law. Indeed, many people sadly either do not see their magic or use it for malevolent purposes (the majority falling into the former category). It is easy to let our egos go untempered and get caught up in the chaos of simply trying to survive modern life. It is easy to forget magic.

But let's align that Law and tap the Realm of Possibility!

The core principles found in the Law can also be found within the five points of the pentacle. Earlier we worked with a simple pentacle microdose cycle. Let's revisit that most ancient magical symbol and use the five points of the star as the five Kabbalistic wisdoms that can aid anyone in aligning the Law. For while the pentacle cycle set out in a previous chapter may seem merely like a simple way to keep a safe dose cycle, there are powers within that symbol that go far deeper.

Pentacles have been important in magic and sacred geometry since the days of Pythagoras (c. 580 – 500 BCE). They were used as signs of protection in Greece and signs of health in Egypt. Each point of the star represents one of four elements: Earth, Wind, Fire, Water; the fifth point signifying Thought (Intellect). Within the Kabbalist Law we might say these five points represent Country (Earth), Community (Water), Friends (Air), Family (Fire), You (Thought/Intellect); these five create the Quintessence – that which is the result of all resting in perfect symphony.

PENTACLE SPELL TO ALIGN THE LAW

On the first day of the pentacle cycle (Thursday, Week 1[1]) I like to set a space with candles and chanting and witchy shit. But, as always, do what speaks to you. I take a threshold dose[2] and follow the meditation→visualization process. Once in that space (visualizing in threshold space) reflect on how respectful you act towards your countryfolk who may not be in the same class, community, or share a similar perspective. Obviously, if someone's perspective is dangerous and cause for alarm that is one thing. But most people, you will find, are pretty good at heart.

Think about your sense of homeland. What are your obligations as a citizen living in your country in the 21st

1. See plate 3.1 in chapter 3.
2. Since this spell includes five spaced-apart days, I prefer a threshold dose. Of course, a microdose works fine too.

century? What about it is worth protecting? What about it protects you? How do you protect it? Write down all the things that you appreciate about your homeland and all the things you do not like about it. Be honest. Your country is, especially in the information age, your daily experience of "Earth."

On the second day of the pentacle cycle (Tuesday, Week 2), take the dose and meditate→visualize on community. What are the values of your community (whether they be social, religious, athletic, political, or otherwise)? What about those values attracted you? Most importantly, how do you treat your rivals in your community, say in a sporting league? Try to see them not as your rivals but as those equally passionate as you. Compete only with yourself. These people, after all, hold (at base) similar values and interests as you. I know this might sound crazy, but if you are well prepared, play at your peak, and still lose the game it is okay to be happy for your opponents. That is the Law.

These communities that we all create are the daily experiences of the Waters on which we sail our ships. We all, too, contribute to the Waters on which others shall sail their ships. We all do this in perfect universe unison when we follow the advice of Mr. D, while consciously tempering the ego.

And so the Law more closely aligns.

On the third day (Saturday, Week 2) take your dose and meditate→visualize on your friends, your immediate group within the community. Do you surround yourself with good people? Do you do favors for your friends without first scheming some kind of reward for your "nice" Action? To return to one of our ego-tempering exercises mentioned earlier, do you owe someone an apology? A *real* apology? These questions (and their *real* answers) are important because, as your Air, your friends are pushing your sails through the Water (and visa-versa). For this fact, this particular pentacle cycle day is as good a day as any to give someone who has been the Air in your sails that *real* apology. Write down all the ways you have both been a good friend and fallen short of the appellation. Be honest. Dishonesty insults the Law and muddles the Four Gifts.

On the fourth day (Tuesday, Week 4) take your dose and meditate→visualize on your family and ask yourself many of the same questions you asked about your friends. Only remember that it was your family that first recognized (and either championed or tried to douse) your Fire. Like it or not, you family represents your origin, and all that you are can be found buried deep in that complex cellular generational mystery of *you*. Best to come to terms with it. Indeed, you even gained from the toxic parts of your family (should there be any), depending on how you reActed and learned from them. Write down all the best and less desirable relationships you have with your family members. If you can think of ways of improving them, taking Action will only serve to compliment the Law.

Finally, on the last day (Saturday Week 4), take your

dose and meditate→visualize on yourself and what you would like to get out of this life. Are you working towards something? If so, do you have a plan? A roadmap? A way to get there? (If not, see chapter 10). You are the ship itself. And a ship must be properly constructed to energetically sail even the roughest waters.

△

Think about the way the immaterial ideas of country funnel down into community, while that material you (with access to magic, of course!) rises up through your friends from your family's origin. Provide for your country, community, friends, and family in a positive way and receive all the benefits of aligning the Law.

For each of these microdose pentacle points (no matter which avenue you create for it) take your dose, meditate→visualize on appointed cycle days, and write down your thoughts both positive and negative. Once you are done, look for the overlaps. As you will no doubt have noticed, this spell acts as a natural pathway, funneling your larger world down to your inner truth. This spell reveals what you value in life. It gives you time to consider a desire or goal you have within the context of your reality.

Most importantly, it acts as a magical bridge to align the Law. ☺

.7.

SIGILS, SHROOMS, AND SEX MAGIC

LET'S GET META-PHYSICAL!

Sigil creation and release is a magical technique that differs from symbols and runes in that they are created solely by you (or a small group) that represent an aspiration. Another difference is that while symbols and runes operate in the conscious past and present, sigils exist in the subconscious present and future. They are used to set intentions, generally a goal of the material kind. Sigils are not small miracles; they are intricate designs of desire. They represent the first *physical* manifestation of an immaterial intention.

Sigils are created with purpose by a person in a relaxed space – the kind of space perfect for meditation and visualization. You can really make your sigil at any time, but I find mornings (especially around 5-6 am) are my preferred times to do any magic. Whether you light candles like me or keep the lights on like you, doesn't matter. Other things that matter not include: incorporating music (which I find distracting); burning incense; or even drawing your sigil while sitting on the toilet. What matters is that you are in a place where you can focus *all* of your intention into this exercise.

Creating and releasing a sigil

1. Take a threshold dose

2. Meditate→visualize your desire.

3. Form a sentence of realistic intention. "I want to win the lottery" and other miracle-thinking nonsense is out! Something more tangible like "I want to find a job that pays more for my talents" is a workable spell. Some even recommend writing the sentence in the affirmative here and now: "I love that my job pays me so much for my talents." The logic is that you do not want to fill your sigil with worry, with which the former sentence, at bottom, is rife. Philosopher Alan Watts called this the "Backwards Law."[1] Watts felt that the more a person recognized that they didn't already have what they wanted the more they created a cycle of

---

1. No relation to the Kabbalistic Law.

worry and doubt in their lives. The Backwards Law is like mentally spinning a steering wheel while hydroplaning—the more you try to gain control of the car the more out of control you spin. This happens because we are making decisions based on avoidance of pain rather than pursuit of pleasure. Therefore, the more you want to "feel" wealthy the more you will recognize your own poverty. Recall that the hardest part is simply trusting in the magic. The trick is to live as if you already have the object of desire. This has very practical everyday applications. A guy who is lonely wants to avoid the pain of loneliness by seeking the pleasure of a lover. The problem is he has become overbearing in his attempts to attract a mate, which (as anyone will tell you) is a big no-no. People are not attracted to desperation; they are attracted to a healthy ordering of the Four Gifts.

4. The next step can be done in any number of ways and orders. I'll just outline three ways in one order so you see what I mean. Let's take the affirmative sentence from above "I love that my job pays me so much for my talents." Beginning with the "l" in "love," remove every other letter from the statement. Now it looks like this:

"I oe ht y o pys e o uh o m tlns."

Time to get rid of those pesky vowels![2]

"ht (y) p(y)s h m tlns."

Sometimes people remove vowels first, then digraphs ("th," "ph," "sh," etc.).

Other times they will extract one letter from the whole sentence to start off. All of these techniques are fine; the point is to get the letters down to a manageable size.

With our manageable size ("ht (y) p(y)s h m tlns") we can now zero-in on what's left that stands out. This will change with each individual. Some might be captivated by the coincidence and beauty of the p(y)s – "psychedelic" combination—*while performing microdosing magic, no less!*—and go for that grouping. Others might find the utter resilience of the "tlns" forces to withstand the punishing blow of second-round vowel annihilation admirable, and choose that group. Still others might go with the simple, esoteric beauty of the "(y)."

Now, take whatever grouping you chose and twist the letters)and parenthesis should they exist(around each other. Stack them on top of each other and twist them again! Do this until they fuse into one unidentifiable *thing.*

That is your sigil.

In this example (plate 7.1) I chose the magically coincidental "p (y) s" combo. I began by writing out "p (y) s" and then stacking the "p" (upside-down) over the "y." I then embellished the endings of the "y"; then I extended the

_____

2. Some people include the "y" with the discarded vowels. Others keep it. I put it in parentheses for aesthetic purposes.

upside-down "p," finally stretching out the "s" and putting it over the entire creation. The result was this sigil.

(Plate 7.1)

You must now release it. Some people choose to release their sigils right away. Others like to wait a week or so before releasing. As ever, do what feels right. Whenever you decide to release the sigil there are both simple and involved ways of doing so. A simple way is to light a candle and meditate on the image of the sigil. Not all that it represents. *Just* the sigil itself. Then take your drawing of the sigil and burn it in the flames.

As outlined in an earlier chapter, I prefer to release a sigil in a state of heightened ecstatic awareness, which can be brought on by dancing, drumming, sex, and/or, of course, a threshold dose of magic mushrooms and deep meditation. Whatever the avenue, you want to release the sigil when your brain is in *that* state—when you are free from thought. Orgasm is a great way to get there. And since that rascally euphoric body high courtesy of the mushrooms is coursing through my body anyway, it's as if the fates have already done half the work for me! So, if you choose the sexual route, a little planning will be involved. Politely ask your partner(s) to leave you to create your sigil and be sufficiently "ready to go" once you have completed it. Or have your partner(s) stay if you prefer—especially if there is a shared goal. In that case, the sigil should be created and released together. Of course this can also be performed autonomously.

The sigil created, embrace each other in the glorious arms of Aphrodite (or yourself in the impish hand of Narcissus); try your best to start focusing on the sigil at the height of orgasm. If you find that too difficult, then try thinking of the sigil as you relish in the afterglow—when your mind is free and clear of everything.

But before you light that cigarette, burn that sigil!

Once the sigil has been burned do not think about it any longer.

It has been released into the Realm of Possibility.

.8.

KEEPERS OF THE PROMETHEAN FLAME
MICRODOSING CREATIVITY SPELLS

"I had expected curiosity and interest on the part of artists outside of medicine—performers, painters, writers," remarked the late, great Albert Hofmann as he reflected on his "problem child," LSD, first synthesized from raw ergot in 1938.[1] The reason for Hofmann's assessment was as obvious back then as it is clear today. LSD—indeed all psychedelics—has proven to engender the remarkable quality of eliciting creative impulses in people. Even the ancient Greeks recognized this form of "divine ecstasy"— the frenzy of inspiration!

---

1. Jonathan Ott (trans.), Albert Hofmann, *LSD: My Problem Child*, pg. 79-80.

Psychedelics manifest their goodies in the space between the firing canons of our neurotransmitters, the synapses. My theory goes that the more creative work one does while in that space, the more a person will see future results with regards to innovation without the aid of any psychedelic.

In any event, I feel it's been working for me. ☺

△

In 1958 George Land had no idea he was beginning a study that would last for a decade. It began as a request from NASA to design a test that asked (roughly speaking): *what makes people creative*? Land developed a simple exam that measured a person's ability to come up with innovative ways to problem solve. Unfortunately, the tests could only tell who was creative *currently*. But this did nothing to answer the question as to whether people were born creative or developed innovative thinking abilities through environment, habits, and experiences picked up over time. Considering the relative easiness with which the test was designed, Land decided to give it to 1,600 five-year-olds.

98% scored in the creative genius category!

The marks dumbfounded the research team. Opting to optimize operational options, Land decided to turn the study into a longitudinal endeavor. The researchers brought the kids back in for testing five years later when they were age 10. In only five years between exams, the kids' scores dropped. Only 30% occupied the creative genius category! Now dumbfounded for a totally new reason, the researchers decided to bring the kids back one more time five years later. At age 15, 12% scored in the creative genius category. But here's the real kicker—Land later tested one million people aged around 31; only 2% scored in the creative genius category.

What happened?! The longitudinal testing answered two questions: first, whether we are born creative geniuses or develop it over time—Land's study would suggest that we are all born naturally creative. And that our natural creativity, somehow, dims over the course of life—and very early in life as well! Furthermore, by the time a healthy person has reached around the quarter of their, her, or his life, this natural creative genius has all but faded into social media scrolling and putting up with negative peoples' shit.

It is no surprise that this decreativitizing happens just as we enter (and exist) school (we begin elementary school at around age 6 or 7 and finish high school around age 18). Through no fault of dedicated and heroic teachers, our education system fleeces us of our creative genius. The problem, astonishingly, is the entire way modern school curriculums are taught; indeed, the curricula force every one of us to use our brains to solve problems in a way that is quite unnatural.

Consider this: our magnificent brains evolved two ways of thinking: the first is called *convergent* thinking. This is the analytical side where we are putting thoughts together consciously and with intention. We judge, plot, scheme, calculate, compute, and make arguments. The second kind of thinking, *divergent* thinking, comprises the free flow thoughts and day dreams; creativity.

And therein lays the problem. Land feels that contemporary education (which is just shy of being 150 years old) encourages us to combine these two ways of thinking when problem solving. This causes a push and pull between fantasy and logic; just as our creative juices start to flow (divergent thinking), our analytical mind tells us useless and nonsensical lies like: "It will never work!" "It's been tried before without success!" and "This is just too impractical!" Such falsehoods cause self-doubt. Self-doubt is not creatively-healthy.

Our Intellect demands we stay creatively healthy. Therefore, instead of merging these two ways of thinking, we ought to be following our weird and loony thoughts (divergent) as far as they can go without interruption (convergent). There are ideas within ideas that expand out of other ideas and we sometimes never get to them because we have already put the brakes on before they get a chance to develop.

There is a way to respark that creative genius.

Indeed, it is sitting in you waiting to hatch!

PSYCHEDELICS AND THE MAGIC OF CREATIVITY

Some of the earliest tests to measure the relationship between creativity and psychedelics began in 1954 when psychiatrist Oscar Janiger ran LSD sessions in southern California. One of his subjects, an artist, had asked the good doctor for some objects to draw. This spawned an idea. Dr. Janiger decided to see how LSD affected the artistic mind, eventually observing and tallying the LSD experiences of sixty professional artists and forty writers and musicians. It was Dr. Janiger himself who referred to artists as "keepers of the Promethean flame."[2] His test, and others like it, concluded with mixed results. While some like Sidney Cohen felt that LSD drowned out external distractions allowing the artist to focus more intently, others concluded that psychedelics "throw open the gates that normally confine our perceptions to familiar territory."[3] Most agreed that while psychedelics enhanced creativity (through whichever avenue) the most noticeable changes manifested *after* the psychedelic's effects had waned. My personal magical experiments with psychedelic creativity spellcasting have drawn similar results. My writing (and output) isn't anything special *during* the creativity spell cycle (though sometimes it is), but is *noticeably* enhanced in the following weeks.

Our creative brains are alive and well, though perhaps simply dormant due to our early experiences of dark sarcasm in the classroom. Therefore, while psychedelics certainly stimulate the mind, we can expedite the process by casting some creative microdosing spells on ourselves!

Since the Moon has long been associated with creation (at

2. Marlene Dobkin de Rios and Oscar Janiger, *LSD: Spirituality and the Creative Process*, pg. 78.
3. Ibid., 80.

least since as long ago as Neolithic fertility religions), I like to use that symbol for short rounds of poetigenic (art magic) cycles. The cycle looks like this (8.1):

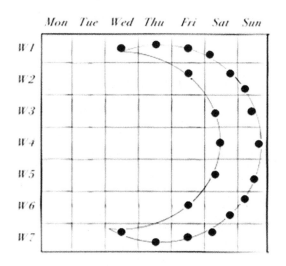

However, I would also like to show you how I extend it outwardly if I find that I am having bursts of innovation (plate 8.2, next page). This emblem is an updated version of that most ancient creative symbolism. It has come to represent general Goddess energy, wedding its association to all creative projects.

You will have noticed that the Pentacle Spell to Align the Law is added to the middle of the circle. You do not necessarily have to add it to the cycle. But if you do, try threshold dosing for those days. I find such stacking offers a crescendo and a landing.

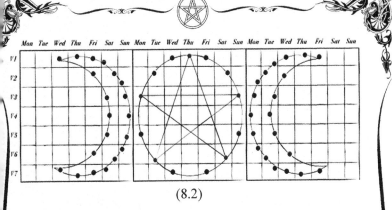

(8.2)

INVOCATION

In the magical world there exist two opinions on the subject of deriving power. Some practitioners abstain from the invocation aspect altogether, feeling this kind of mumbo-jumbo gets in the way of magic (that for them usually goes no further than psychology). Others rely solely on divine intervention by a Goddess or God or some other spiritually advanced entity to do most anything. The former practitioners usually see the latter as little more than time-wasting kooks fooled by their own imagination. The latter tend to feel the former are self-centered "gods" of their own universe … equally fooled by their own imagination.

My particular magical system finds value in both perspectives. I believe that there exist forces both inside (The Three Spiritual Forces) and outside myself (gravity, seasonal change, love). The ancient Greeks believed in inspiration as a force outside the self. One can easily relate to this principle. I am neither a painter nor a photographer, but I am often inspired to capture a beautiful sunset on either a canvas or on film. Something outside myself (a sunset) has a remarkable effect on me aesthetically. I may create from *within*, but I am inspired from *without*.

As such, I invoke. When I plan to do any kind of poetigenic magic during a creativity spell cycle it is my way to first invoke the Muses.

Invoking the Muses keeps me on task and focused. I am under a spell. If I start to waste my time dicking around on social media I remember that something terrible will happen if I break a spell—the Muses may cut my vocal chords and transplant them to a more worthy receiver! To avoid such unpleasantness, I offer:

A SPELL TO INVOKE THE MUSES

1. Since the Muses love flowers of all kinds, I do not perform a proper banishing. Instead, I scatter pink and white flower petals as a way to suck up any negative energies that may be lurking about. I spread the petals in my room outlining a pentacle (*naturally*) in lieu of using incense. I pay no mind to how the petals fall (i.e., I don't spend all my time trying to create the perfect pentacle on the floor).

2. Take microdose and meditate→visualize the part of the project I wish to tackle over the next few days/ weeks.

3. Using a bundle of wheat or twigs, I make a pentacle

in the air before me, saying three times (getting louder each round), "Adjuri, Muses, Dearte! Anima mea intrant!" ("I adjure you, Muses. Enter my soul!")

4. I take Action!

TRY USING YOUR FEET! (THIS IS YOUR BRAIN ON DRUGS)

For every day during the cycle(s) posted above, try doing one or more of the following:

1. Take your dose and meditate→visualize. Once you are visualizing, beginning with your body, envisage all the things you have to do that day *with special focus on the hand you will use to accomplish them.* Then simply go through (visualize) your usual day. When you use your non-dominant hand to perform ordinary tasks (write, grill a burger, finger your butthole) you stimulate your entire brain (as opposed to doing things with your dominant hand which only stimulates one side of your brain).

What are the normal things you do daily with your dominant hand? For everyone's sake, I hope you brush your teeth! Switch hands. I like to brush my teeth after the threshold dose and morning meditation→visualization magic using my left (non-dominant) hand. (One of the things I noticed while getting used to brushing with my non-dominant hand was that I, at first, held the toothbrush in a death grip. I found that easing up and relaxing my shoulder helped immensely.) Then there are other things like using an ATM or even *dialing* a number if you have to make a phone call.

2. On your way to work, while listening to a podcast or music you can enjoy the soft pleasure of twiddling your thumbs. Or you can bring a small notepad with you and write down what you are listening to … with your non-dominant hand. Remember, magic exists between spaces and it is in those spaces where we do our magical training so that we can do our best magical work! Sitting on a bus, train, or in a traffic jam provides just such spaces! So use that time wisely.

If I am listening to music, I jot down the lyrics of the songs with my left hand. If I am listening to a podcast, I just jot down as many words as possible; if I miss some, that's fine. That's not the point. The point is neurogenesis—and when mixed with mushrooms, it does wonders for the creative soul!

3. An easy one is simply moving your computer mouse to the non-dominant side. I have been doing this one for several months at the time of this

writing. At one point, my brain literally cracked and I had to get up from my desk and walk it off! But I got the hang of it more and more with each passing day and invite you to give it a shot.

4. Try to recall things before looking them up (say on your space phone). Too often I would find myself looking at my watch or phone to check the time … only to look three seconds later! I decided not to go immediately back to my phone; I would first think about the time for about *5-10 seconds*. What I discovered was I remembered most of the time! You can do this with anything, really. If you look something up and then forget it, don't automatically reach for your space phone. Try to remember it first. Then, if you truly cannot (give it at *least* a minute), look it up again.

5. Learn a song you are familiar with in another language ("Happy Birthday" works great—there are numerous versions!)

6. Try using your feet! If you are at home and drop a utensil or receipt or anything on the floor, channel your inner primate and try grabbing those kinds of things with your toes on your non-dominant foot.

7. Gematria – gematria is the practice of bringing usually unconnected topics into correlation by adding letters, words, and phrases into unnatural

relation. Some magicians poo-poo gematria as an illegitimate technique because of the arbitrary way the letters and terms are arranged (i.e., confirmation bias).[4] While I agree with that sentiment, I still think gematria is useful not so much as a magical technique but as a creativity technique.

We exist in a world of don'ts ("Don't put pineapple on a pizza," "don't wear mismatched socks," "girls wear pink; boys wear blue," and, fearing Serial Mom, "do not wear white shoes after labor day!"). We have our little boxes of familiarity and rarely do those boxes spill into the other.

And yet, many great inventions we know about usually come from two (or more), seemingly unrelated, origins. Let's take everyone's favorite travel convenience: roller luggage. Today, we can't imagine an airport not filled with busy people rushing to catch their flights with their own personal luggage carts rolling faithfully behind them. But where were these little marvels only forty years ago? They didn't exist yet. *Someone* thought of it. *Someone* put two totally unrelated ideas (luggage and transportation) and merged it into something many of us can't live without. That someone is Bernard D. Sadow, a now retired vice president of a luggage and coat company in Massachusetts.

4. IAO 131, *Naturalistic Occultism.* pg. 81-3.

One *simple* idea, one *desire* for a better way (no matter how small) turned Sadow into a multimillionaire and made travel easier for us all.

To conclude on gematria: the following goes against every principle of historical criteria that I believe in, but: *start making unnatural and seemingly unrelated correlations between shit!*

ADVANCED!

1. Try wiping your ass with the other hand.
    Have soap ready.

2. Make up an alternative personality for yourself and live as that person for one day. Use an accent, a made-up background, Emotional scars—*everything*. A bar provides the perfect theater for this creativity spell.

3. When you are waiting (on line, for public transit, etc.) do not reach for your phone. Instead, come up with a short story in your head. If you have to start off with a very short tale, that's cool—there is plenty of waiting around in life! Add to the story as time goes on if you see fit.

4. When you plug an address into your GPS, don't actually follow it. Simply look at the roads/turns, whathaveyou, and memorize the route.

(Warning: make sure you are not annoying the shit out of yourself with all of this!)

▽

Electronic technology rocks! But do not ever let it replace that most glorious, intricate, divine mind you have sitting in the confines of your brain that is constantly channeling magic into the Realm of Possibility! O, sweet keeper of the Promethean flame, your mind is the greatest playground ever evolved!

Play, for heaven's sake! Play!

These brain exercises coupled with micro- and threshold dosing stimulate your creative mind. You should notice the effects of this spell in the weeks that follow termination of the cycle—(although you will certainly see the benefits during the cycle as well!).

This is your brain on drugs.

Any questions?

Looking Forward to Monday

A microdosing teamwork spell
for bands, artists, athletes, and
entrepreneurs

A hint[1] of controversy arises around the use of psychedelics to improve society through entrepreneurialism. Extreme conservatives may feel that "drugs" have no place in business, while hardcore leftists tend to see business cultures as inherently "evil" and therefore not worthy of the lessons garnered through even psychedelia lite. As in most cases of mutually exclusive extremism, both sides are missing too much of the picture to form a valid conclusion on this topic.

"With psychedelics, if you're fortunate and break through,

1. To put it mildly.

you understand what is truly of value in life. Material, power, dominance, and territory have no value. People wouldn't fight wars, and the whole system we have currently would fall apart. People would become peaceful, loving citizens, not robots marching around in the dark with all their lights off."[2]

- Gary Fisher

Maybe.

I think it important to dispel the myth of psychedelics as magic bullets for peace, love, and understanding. Can psychedelics lead to these kinds of revelations? Absolutely! But as medicine hunter Chris Kilham would say, "not all visions are wise."[3] For example, in the early 1980s, Suzan and Michael Carson, who took copious amounts of LSD and magic mushrooms, decided the best use of their time was to start a bastard form of Islam that advocated killing witches living in San Francisco![4] Even today the so-called Ayahuasca tourism industry of the Amazon remains troubled by a minority of malevolent sorcerers who, instead of healing their patients, drug, rape, and sometimes even murder them.

The problem with Fisher's assessment is that *all* ancient psychedelics-using peoples (Egyptians, Greeks, Sumerians, etc.) were domination civilizations. The cannabis-smoking Thracians were also among the most warlike peoples of the ancient world. Thracian women were

2. Gary Fisher quoted on Psychedelic Quotes; accessed via: thethirdwave.co/psychedelic-quotes/
3. Chris Kilham, "Not All Visions are Wise," presented at Spirit Plant Medicine Conference, 4, November, 17.
4. See Richard D. Reynolds, *Cry for War: The Story of Suzan and Michael Carson* (CA: Walnut Creek, Squibob Press, 1987).

such fierce and skilled warriors that the Greeks could only interpret their ferocity mythologically, creating tales of the "Amazons." When the Thracian king died (say in battle) his people smoked oodles of cannabis in religious ceremony while burying him. This entheogenic rite was *hardly* anti-establishment. Additionally, as scholars have persuasively argued (and I count myself among them) an entheogen of some kind was at play in the Eleusinian Mysteries of ancient Greece. The ancient Greeks (to say nothing of their Mycenaean precursors who founded these rites) were *anything* but peaceful. And their form of "democracy" represents a mere philosophical speck of what it means to us today. And what of the Egyptians? For all their vast knowledge of entheogenic plants they were still among the richest slave-driving peoples in the ancient world. The peyote-eating Aztec priests? Eating *teonanácatl* ("god's flesh") didn't stop them from ripping the still-beating hearts out of prisoners to please Huitzilopochtli, the sun god.

Further examples from history could be quadrupled over and over.

So why is Fisher mistaken? A simple anachronism: *our* modern paradigm places the psychedelic experience at the heart of non-conformity. Why? Because our first experiences in the modern world—our first cultural paradigms with things like LSD, mushrooms, cannabis, etc.— show us this very picture (despite the fact that they have been used for thousands of years to *uphold* the status quo). Our current psychedelic paradigm is bolstered by two fractious sub-paradigms, both myopic in scope. The first sub-paradigm (the conservative side), gives you politicians of every aisle telling you that psychedelics will ruin your life. The second sub-paradigm (the liberal side) is our inheritance from the hippies and the Antiwar Movement of the late 1960s. The short of it is this: war, death, pain, destruction are all *bad* things. The hippies, who epitomized the opposite (perpetual indulgence of life) represented the inverse of war, death, pain, etc. Because of these two sub-paradigms clashing into each other in 20th century American popular culture, many of our friends today remain unaware of how *new* the "we are all oneness" of psychedelia is.

Until the 1960s, most psychedelic experiences were couched in cultures that were all about power, dominance, and territory (save medieval fertility goddess religions and the rare Maria Sabinas of the world ... *who still charged a fee for their services*—Oh No!). The Vietnam War and Antiwar Movement—the dynamic friction between the conservative and liberal views—are what actually created the "we are all oneness" of the modern psychedelic experience. There are few traces of that paradigm in history before then. "Love thy neighbor" used to mean just *that*— love for your neighbor. Those not in your neighborhood? *Fuck 'em*!

But as we enter a more "global" civilization we have to start rethinking that paradigm.

We can trace much of this muddle to the 1960s and

its grandstanding gadfly, Timothy Leary, who encouraged young people to eat acid and "turn on, tune in, and drop out." The businessperson recoiled ("Drop out of society?!?! Then who will buy my useless crap?!"); and the hippie rejoiced in apathy ("Society had a good run, man."). Two paradigms that had never existed in history (i.e., "psychedelics are inherently bad for society" (extreme right) and "psychedelics are inherently bad for society—*good*" (extreme left) began to form, poisoning the well of historical psychedelia just as we were rediscovering our long lost roots.

It was Leary's last admonition ("drop out") that has caused such discord in our day. Indeed, even casual observation would suggest that we are not engaging the Kabbalistic societal Law as much as we probably should. Dropping out is certainly not an answer. Maybe filling the system with creative, compassionate people will make a more profound and lasting difference?

And yet others feel differently. Psychedelics researcher and educator Jonathan Thompson questions microdosing because for him, that's not what psychedelia is all about. While acknowledging the benefits of sporadic microdosing, Thompson favors the "life changing experience" of the psychedelic and hero doses more so than smaller doses "akin to a daily pharmaceutical which is taken to increase productivity and effectiveness in the working world." While I respect my friend's perspective, in my opinion he seems to be operating under the paradigm that psychedelics are, as he put it, "inherently anti-establishment, anti-materialistic."[5] But we must recall that this paradigm is only half a century old, so it's easy to assume that things have always been this way. Before the 1960s, psychedelics were very much used to uphold the establishment. Heart-tearing Aztec peyote priests—to say nothing of the Greek priestesses who dished out the psychedelic kykeon potion at Eleusis—hardly constituted counter-cultures.

They comprised the status-quo.

▽

I think back to 2011 when I lived in Long Beach, NY, and the Occupy movement erupted. Back then it wasn't an Occupy "movement" yet; it was Occupy Wall Street. The message, as comedian Jon Savoy noted, was that "our government holds allegiance to companies that hold no allegiance to the United States." At the time, I ran a small private education business with a friend of mine, catering to wealthy north shore Long Islanders—the very people who worked on Wall Street. I decided to use the money I made to buy goods and supplies (food, women's products, toiletries, etc.) and dispense them freely among the people at Zuccotti Park, where the movement began.

Look, I'm not exactly sure what was happening in those days. Such economic circumstances remain above my pay-grade. What I was sure of was that my business

---

5. Jonathan Thompson; pers. comm.

did hold allegiance to the United States and its beautiful countryfolk. And that its beautiful countryfolk looked tired, worried, and hungry. Money isn't really evil, intentions are. And since we are *not* going to overthrow the free market we may as well see if we can't make that system work better for us.

So I propose a possible new paradigm!

In the event that some good can come from psychedelic entrepreneurialism I would like to share a system (called "roadmapping") that many companies have found useful. Only we are going to add a little microdosing magic to the mix!

Roadmapping is a process of establishing themes. It can be done for businesses, art projects, theater productions, bands, festival planning—anything, really! Feel free to use the following roadmapping system and accompanying microdose cycle and see how it works for your team.

The purpose of this spell is nothing short of collective creation to better society.

PREP WORK

First you must decide who should be on the roadmapping team. While there are no hierarchies within the roadmapping system, there does have to be an initial organizer that gets everyone together. The group works best when kept around 4 – 6 people (all with specific knowledge needed in a certain area pertaining to the project).

Request that each participant of the roadmap session run a microdose cycle that keeps the intake of the mushrooms neutral. A good cycle symbol is the hexagram for several reasons: firstly (and most pragmatically), there are seven questions incorporated into the roadmap system. Secondly, seven is a magical number: it is both Apollo the sun god's number (and we are *always* curving towards the sun!) and the designation of a person who sees their, her, or his dreams to the end (i.e. a "7 percenter").

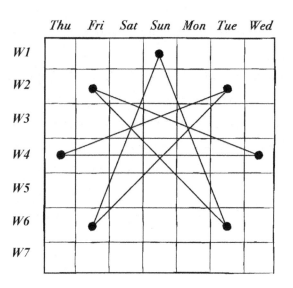

The first three questions have a specific order to be asked that optimizes the results of reaching answers come the roadmap session. Those questions are:

1. Where do we want to go? (Vision)

2. Where are we now? What present realities do we have to use (material)?

3. How do we get there? What is the plan to accomplish this (immaterial)?

The next four questions are the SWOT questions:

4. What are the <u>S</u>trengths of this idea?

5. What are the <u>W</u>eaknesses of the idea?

6. What are the *real* <u>O</u>pportunities?

7. What are the <u>T</u>hreats/potential setbacks?

On dose day 1 (Sunday, Week 1) take your dose in the morning and meditate→visualize on this, and only this, first above question. Do the same for doses two and three (Friday and Tuesday of Week 2), and then take a week break from dosing and thinking about those three questions (obviously, if you come up with something ingenious during the off week, do not hesitate to add it to your notes!). After the week off, finish the cycle meditating→visualizing the four SWOT questions, taking the doses on the appointed hexagram cycle days.

Microdosing and the seven pillars of wisdom

Another reason I prefer this particular cycle (the hexagram) for roadmapping to begin on Sunday has to do with the astrological association of certain days. When put together with roadmapping, a secret story reveals itself: that of the wedding of the Sun and the Moon through mastery of the Seven Pillars of Wisdom. And while the ancients gendered their astrological signs, for this spell they shall remain gender-neutral.

<u>Sunday</u> – (Sun) represents the ego, the dreams of the individual within the group. It is the vessel of enjoyment for which our consciousness plays. Our ego is our container for our unique slice of the cosmos. It is our paintbrush, our lifeline to all that exists; there is no magic, no growth, without ego. Only we want to keep our ego in the mental Goldilocks' zone: not too hot not too cold, but *jjjuuusstttttt* right! On this day, try one of the ego-tempering exercises shared in an earlier chapter.

For the Sun holds the Pillar of the Wisdom of Tempered Ego.

<u>Friday</u> (Venus) – harmony, solidarity, and unity. Today reflect on the virtues of the team members and why they were picked. If you are on the team but did not pick the members, think about all the virtues and good qualities they bring to the table. Even if you don't necessarily like them. Actually, *especially* if you don't necessarily like them. You are all working on this project for the same reason. You need each other. Today is always a good day to swallow one's pride and reach out to that person(s) and say that you are looking forward to creating something positive and

beautiful with them. If you get along with everyone on the team, write them a love letter. *Send it*!

For Venus holds the Pillar of the Wisdom of Love and Cooperation.

Tuesday (Mars) – assertion, ambition, drive. What are the things you have already accomplished in your life? Do you play a musical instrument? In your mind, go back to the first day you picked up, say, a guitar. You sucked. It was frustrating, and difficult, and at times you wanted to give up … but here you are, all these years later, shredding away at the neck for leisure. How about a language? A sport? A skill? Get in touch with it this day.

For Mars holds the Pillar of the Wisdom of Determination.

Thursday (Jupiter) – governs growth and material wealth. Jupiter rules business endeavors. I like to use this time to reflect on fairness. What will I do to make sure that anyone who buys a book, takes a course, or hears me speak publically feels they got their money's worth? How will I be a worthy investment of their time? Or what about an athletic event? Am I fully trained and prepared to compete at the level of my teammates and competitors when I lace up my skates? How will I make sure I put the work in?

For Jupiter holds the Pillar of the Wisdom of Worthiness.

Wednesday (Mercury) the messenger. What is the message

you want to share with your community through your project? How does it fit in with the larger world? What language will you use to communicate it? Mercury also rules adaptability and versatility, ipso facto it is by nature a day conducive to flow.

For Mercury holds the Pillar of the Wisdom of Communication.

Saturday (Saturn) – Commitment, loyalty, dedication, production, intention, endurance. This particular microdosing roadmap spell already seems so involved, and yet, we have only just begun! Your project, whatever it may be, reflects a similar, arduous process. If nothing good comes easy, then everything great comes from following the example of Saturn.

For Saturn holds the Pillar of the Wisdom of Patience.

Monday (Moon) – The moon symbolizes creation and fresh beginnings and new life. Whether that new beginning be a startup, theater production, interior design, recording an album, or automotive engine building project. How will you handle this new endeavor? With old assumptions or with new ones? How will you handle discord (should it arise) between team members during the process?

For the Moon holds the Pillar of the Wisdom of Creation.

The ego has now gone through seven stages of wisdom so as to reach the moment of manifestation. When put together in that order, they tell a story:

You must recognize your ego's place (Sunday) within your roadmapping group (Friday) while driving forward (Tuesday) propelled by worthiness (Thursday) through clear communication (Wednesday) and commitment (Saturday) to manifest the heretofore immaterial outcome (Monday).

It's time to start looking forward to Monday! ☺

(TA)ROADMAPPING

To further optimize this spell let's add a little more magic by implementing a few tarot principles to roadmap thinking. Tarot is a magical tradition stemming back to the late 1700s that uses cards to map out possible future outcomes to a specific question. The cards first entered Europe in the late 1300s from the East as an ordinary deck used for a game called "Triumph." It was not until 1791 that Protestant minister Antoine Court de Gebelin (also a Freemason) gave each card of the tarot deck an occult meaning. Eventually, reading tarot cards became a huge hit with eccentric aristocrats who wanted to know what the future held for them. Several mental magical techniques ultimately joined the art, and by the post-Victorian era the magical tarot had swept many upper-class occult circles.

Reading tarot is a far more complicated endeavor than what I have planned for this short spellbook. It is as circuitous as the Kabbalist Tree of Life and requires as much study and discipline. But the mental magical techniques that accompany tarot, I think, are pure gold and can be applied to this, or really any, microdosing spell.

These tarot mental magical techniques include:

POSITIVITY: all magic begins with a positive outlook on the situation. Even questions that may seem like negatives can be reframed in a positive future context. For example, question 5 may be asked retrospectively as, "What did I recognize needed strengthening?"

DON'T OVER COMPLICATE: when thinking about these questions, do not get bogged down in technicalities and complexity; you aren't doing these initial magical exercises to determine every possible scenario and solve all the problems. This is a *creative* space. Eschew details for a free flow of ideas. Remember, *Divergent thinking > Convergent thinking!*

NEUTRALITY: you want to remain in a neutral, judgment-free, headspace. It is quite difficult to not judge thoughts that seem outlandish. With roadmapping there will be idea-sharing once the group session commences and this simple principle helps you remain both open with your own ideas, and more importantly, open to the ideas of others. So, for the sake of this spell, allow those crazy thoughts to form and unfold where they want to go. This will not necessarily awaken your subconscious, but it will touch upon that liminal, magical space between waking and dreaming where anything is possible.

All this prep-work is done to stir your immaterial memories and turn them into physical signs of Emotion. Emotions can be very powerful when focused (consider a songwriter pouring her guts into lyrics that one day becomes a hit song), so harnessing their natural energy helps any creative endeavor.

Now it's time to roadmap!

THE SESSION

Plan a meeting with your team a week after you all complete the above exercises (it is very important that you all stick to the same days and doses; you want to all stay magically in sync – you are going to be "holding space" for each other for literally weeks!). Have everyone bring sticky notes and a pen or two. It also helps to have a neutral facilitator to keep time so that all members (bosses, directors, producers) are a part of the team working together. You'll also need a roadmap board on which to post the notes. The board I modeled this spell on is very general. I encourage each team to lookup different roadmap boards (a simple web search fetches plenty) and work with one that best suits the specific needs of the project. Begin the session having all members doing our trusty meditation→visualization technique. Let the individual fires of this method cross-pollinate the energy around the team.

The first question the facilitator should ask is "why do we want to do this?" Give 5 minutes for everyone to write their answers and name on a sticky note. Write as many answers as possible, and post them on the board.

Question 2a is "What is our vision?" What is the general idea of what you all hope to do? Again, give five minutes to dream-up and post ideas. Question 2b asks the definable objectives: what do we have to do to accomplish [x, y, and z]?

At this point take a 15-20 minute break.

When the break ends, back to meditation→visualization, but for only 20 minutes total (ten minutes of both). Return to questions.

Question 3 asks "what is the current state?" What is the state you are working in? The cultural climate? The business climate? In what weather are you setting out to sea? What resources do you have? What resources do you need?

Question 4: What are the steps to the vision? Get into story-telling mode. Have everyone close their eyes, return to their visualization awareness, and come up with their own story of how the team got from where it started to accomplishing the vision. Put yourselves in the future, looking back on the past. How did you finish the project? If it helps, try framing the development of the story within the tale of how the Sun went through the Seven Pillars of Wisdom (ego-tempering, community, ambition, growth, intention, commitment, and creation) to wed the Moon.

Develop vivid imagery.

Question 5: What do you intend to learn from all of this? How will you show your progress? How do you share the future of the project?

For each of these questions, do not block any creativity at all, but remain 100% focused on solutions—even seemingly outlandish ones. Anyone can be creative in a supporting environment; at any moment mental-lighting can strike!

Hold that space.

The roadmap session usually takes about two to three hours. But it is two to three hours of everyone in the room fully engaged with solving a problem that they have already been thinking about with their magical minds for a few weeks. During the roadmap session portion, ideas fully charged *pop* from all the magical prep-work!

△

Perhaps the answer may not be "tear down the system." It just *may be* instead fill the system with creative and compassionate folks.

Now that's societal magic on a *grand scale*!

.10.

<u>THRESHOLD DOSE SPELL I USED TO QUIT COFFEE</u>

PSYCHEDELICS FOR MINOR ADDICTIONS

𝒜s more and more people discover the benefits of psychedelics the question of addiction treatment quickly comes to the fore. The plants which seem to hold the most promise are Ibogaine and Ayahuasca. Sadly, like those most magical mushrooms, these magical and medicinal plants remain illegal as well. Happily, the tide seems to be currently turning towards the side of good and we are already seeing greater acceptance of these medicines in society.

I agree with Jonathan Thompson as to the

importance of the higher doses when it comes to major addictions. Perhaps the most remarkable plant to enter psychedelic conversations with regards to addiction is Ibogaine. Karen O' Neel, an advocate of Ibogaine use to treat bulimia, feels that Ibogaine "resets you" to a time "before you had any addictions."[1] From there, it is up to you to not relapse (although this isn't always as easy as it sounds). Karen needed two Ibogaine "floods" (as these deep sessions are called) to free her from bulimia. But she hasn't purged in 7 months (at the time of this writing) which, as she said was "pretty much a freaking miracle." A few deaths have been reported from Ibogaine, but they are the result of undiagnosed heart conditions or using harder drugs like benzos, meth, or prescription opiates within a few days after the flood. These entheogens are fairly safe when used in a responsible setting by facilitators well practiced in administering them. I am not a facilitator of this kind so I will not address how to use them in psychedelic magic. Though, if you do suffer from hard addictions like eating disorders or heroin, please consider looking into finding the right facilitator for you.

Indeed, these medicines work wonders!

Other things like Ayahuasca helped noted author Graham Hancock quit his dependence on cannabis. I have personally been there myself. And while I have heard that cannabis is not technically addictive, that was not my experience. In fact, I found that I used that excuse

---

1. Karen O' Neel, "Beating Bulimia with Ibogaine," presented for the Portland Psychedelic Society, 10, May, 2018.

("cannabis isn't addictive") to smoke more cannabis! However, I have also found that the more I restrict my cannabis use to spiritual practice (i.e., enthogenic use) the more enjoyable and profound the experiences are for me.

Cannabis aside, I do not suffer from any major addictions. Things just didn't turn out that way for me. I did however manage to kick my little pedestrian addiction to coffee through threshold dose magic. Coffee is as benign a "drug" a person will find, and yet there are a number of benefits that have made it worthwhile for me to give it up. My teeth and my breath both got much brighter (which was good considering all the yawning I was doing from microdosing). I saved money—a lot of it! I was dependent on one fewer thing. I was far less jittery during the day and really mellowed out. And, best of all, after a while waking up and getting out of bed was both pleasant and desirable!

By complete coincidence, I quit drinking coffee on January 1st, 2018, after one of the most horrific half-life-long addictions one can have to the devil's bean. To illustrate: I put four or five cups of coffee into one machine and drank the entire thing.

Twice a day.

Three if I had a book due.

I had no intention, no New Year resolution whatsoever, to quit coffee. I see it as a totally unforeseen byproduct of the New Year Ascension Spell outlined in an earlier chapter. I just so happened to wake up on January 1st around 4-5 pm and knew that if I had coffee I would be up all night again. So I smoked a few bowls, dicked around, and went back to sleep fairly early. I had done it. *One* day without coffee!

I woke up around 4:30-5 am the next day. I couldn't recall a time that I didn't have a vat of coffee within minutes of waking up. In that moment, I decided to do something that still surprises me to this day: instead of making coffee, I went for a jog. A quick jog – just to wake up a little. It worked. Sort of. The post-jog shower also helped. But not for long. I decided to eat a threshold dose of mushrooms. After all, it was very early and I did not have to start my day for a few hours. Perhaps if I just relaxed and let the effects wane I'd have that "post trip" energy, I reasoned. I had time to kill, so I took a threshold dose and just went back to lying around in bed—it was far easier to resist having coffee this way. When the dose took effect, I just lay there with my eyes closed and let it wash all over me. An hour or so later it was just about 8 am. The sun was shining and when I got out of bed *this time*, I was surprisingly okay. In fact, I was better than okay! I had energy. But it was different from coffee energy; it felt more natural. After a full day of work, the caffeine crash nonetheless caught up with me. I simply abided to it and took it easy that evening. By the time I went to bed, I couldn't believe what I had just accomplished. *Two* days without coffee! From that point on, it became a test of Will.

At the time of this writing it has been seven months and I am still coffee-less. I will, every now and then (during "off season") have a cup of tea. But I find that I can take it or leave it. And that is miles away from the meat-hooks of caffeine that once tore through my flesh!

I eventually developed a spell (as I am want to do) around this process that I'd like to share with you. Using threshold dosing to quit a minor addiction like coffee is best saved for days you have off from work (a week works best) so as to dedicate all your time to this magical, transformative process. Also, you need to have things to fill your time during this process or it will be excruciating! Any home projects, personal or otherwise, are good to have on tap here. Hell—binge watching the *Lord of the Rings Trilogy* several times works just as well as fixing a sink.

For this spell I use what I call the "four sacred teachers" (cannabis, mandrake, henbane, mushrooms). Feel free to use other plants, herbs, fungi if these do not speak to you.

Rest assured, there are no correct or incorrect ways of quitting coffee.

But this is how I did it.

ADJURATION TO GAIA

Wake up early in the morning without an alarm clock by going to bed early the night before (take however many hours you need to wake up naturally at around cockcrow).

Eat a threshold dose and then light some incense and, using a smudge stick of sage and evergreen, banish the room by making a large pentacle of smoke, purifying the air.

1. Light a coal and place it in a small cauldron, which is placed on an altar.

2. Take a pinch of mandrake and drop it on the burning coal saying, "I offer you [Gaia] mandrake to keep in my heart the lessons of the past." Using a wheat bundle (symbolizing creation and growth), lightly move the fumes three times upward.

3. Next, take a pinch of cannabis and drop it on the burning coal saying, "I offer you cannabis to recognize in my heart the lessons of the present." (Repeat wheat bundle movement three times.)

4. Drop a pinch of psilocybin on the burning coal saying, "I offer you fungus to remind my heart that my ideal 'future' exists today." (Repeat wheat bundle movement three times.)

5. Then a pinch of henbane dropped on the burning coal saying, "I offer you henbane to cycle good magic throughout my journeys." (Repeat wheat bundle movement three times.)

6. Drip spit or blood[2] onto the burning coal saying, "I offer

---

2. I use dental floss to cut the gum between my back teeth to draw this particular magical juice.

you my essence. For my body is a temple of light, fearing and practicing no evil." (Repeat wheat bundle movement three times.)

7. Then, use wheat bundle to draw a pentacle in the air after each word:

"My Intention" (draw pentacle), "My Will" (draw pentacle), "my Path" (draw pentacle), "and my Outcome" (draw pentacle); (arms now stretch out) "Align like the Royal Stars of Night." This is done three times.

8. Then get back into bed and just lay around until you feel the urge to get up again (usually about an hour or so).

9. Get up and do something active. My preferred method is dancing to "Land of a Thousand Dances." (It doesn't matter *what* you do, just do something active immediately.)

10. Then go right to work on whatever project (in my case, writing one of my books or unclogging my bathroom sink).

As soon as I felt the caffeine crash hitting me, I simply repeated the process:

1. Threshold Dose.

2. Adjuration to Gaia.

3. Back in bed for an hour or so.

4. Out of bed into immediate, quick activity (dancing, jogging, roller skating, etc.).

5. Back to the project.

▽

You must dedicate yourself at least a week to this process, which probably means sacrificing a vacation from work.

Spring break will have to wait.

During this particular spell there is absolutely no cycle schedule. Take the threshold dose whenever the time arises to repeat this process (it will be different for everyone). Pay absolutely no mind to keeping yourself awake during this procedure. When you feel the need to rest, stop working and repeat the steps above. Take the catnaps you require during the day. Be lazy as shit. Have all friends and loved-ones stay *ffaarrrrrrr* away from you. Go to bed early if need be (but not before 9 pm – I found 10 pm to be *perfect*). Do not interrupt your body's process. It is relearning the dynamic between "asleep" and "awake" without caffeine. Do not at any moment commit the blasphemy of interrupting your rest with an alarm clock!

Obligate yourself to this process for one week.[3]

It is doubtful you will ever need coffee again.

I certainly don't. ☺

---

3. When you do go back to work in a week, a threshold dose in the early morning or a microdose during the day as a "pick me upper" may be helpful.

.11.

*O*FF SEASON
KEEPING UP WITH MAGICAL PRACTICE

What to do in between microdose spell cast cycles (i.e., the "off-season")? I think a good use of the off-season is to work with threshold doses once or twice in a month. You might also consider (if the threshold dose is not your jam) developing your own magical rituals that carry your microdosing work into the off-season. Remember that the dose is only a *fraction* of the magic. The following spells were developed in conjunction. They can be performed separately, but I find they have the most impact when cast together.

Witchy Baptism (bring toilet paper!)

The witchy baptism is a moon spell usually done in conjunction with the following sun spell (see below). I personally think these microdelic spells work best with couples, both those going through rocky times and those who wish to keep their romance interesting.

Now I should warn you. This spell was originally designed as a fast track to witchyness for those who desired a no restriction, balls-deep dive into the natural craft. As such it remains. But this spell should not be taken as a substitution for actual practice whatsoever. So be careful! If you perform this rite, and it *speaks* to you, please consider further practice into the craft of natural witchyness (and try the following spell, Sunshine up Your Ass!, in conjunction with this one). On the other claw, if this ritual does not speak to you – you'll still have a fun story to tell at a cocktail party!

Ritual preparation (*DIETA*)

This is one of the few spells I do that require a *dieta* (a preliminary diet). But like all spells in this book, the *dieta* is not strict; however, it is *necessary* for the spell.

You'll need:
1. A large meal.
2. Some good cannabis.
3. Toilet paper.

This meal can be anything, preferably something high in protein. Usually for me, it is a large, greasy bar burger and a beer because the point of this ritual is a back-end purge. A bar burger and a beer usually do it for my tiny, starving-artist stomach; that is, of course, unless the ritual just so happens to fall on taco Tuesday.

The cannabis is necessary because of the way it relaxes the innards after a large meal. For we aren't just going to "loosen the girders of the soul," but also summon the pixies of the bowels! And while I no longer drink coffee I can highly recommend a "hippy speedball" (mixing coffee with cannabis) to achieve these ends—the cannabis loosens the flow of righteous poop while the coffee makes most rapid haste discharging the warm turds.

So on a fine summer day, I eat my greasy bar burger, drink my beer, and retreat into the woods. As a city kitty, going into the wilderness represents part of the ordeal for me. It signifies the seriousity of my intentions. But if you live in a quiet area you can probably do it somewhere near your house. I prefer to get far away from civilization – at least half a mile off the beaten path (and leave my space phone at home, or at least in the car). I hike into the woods, find a flat area and outline a circle with sticks, branches, clumps of dirt, leaves, fallen pine needles, etc. I then trace a pentacle that touches five areas of the circle, removing all large and/or sharp rocks. I light sage and evergreen (but, ya know, use whatever you like ☺) and trace around the circle and the star with the smoke. Finally, I dig a hole in the middle of the star.

I then take all my clothes off. Everything – sneakers too. Here I like to have an intention—perhaps some kind of minor habit I am looking to purge. I then roll around on the ground, making sure to splotch the star within the circle all over my body. I get the dirt, leaves, sticks, whatever all over me. I then smoke a bowl, stand over the hole I dug that now sits solo in the circle, and meditate on the purge. For me anyway, cannabis works rather effectively as a natural laxative after a large meal by loosening the muscles (ginger also works well if you prefer a non-psychedelic prompt). I squat and defecate into the hole. Wipe, and put the toilet paper into the hole with it. Cover it with dirt.

There exists an occult duality beneath this seemingly-gratuitously revolting spell. We are, by and large, grossed out by feces (except for those people that get off on it). But here you are making art, making *magic*, with your bodily surplus in a totally healthy, nontoxic way. It's an act of radical acceptance of the most undesirable thing about you: your poop. It is a way of turning the smelliest, shadowyest part of you, your poop, into magic.

Post defecation I wash myself in a river or stream. I let the dirt and mud and such pull any negative buildups that I may still be holding out of my pores and let the waters wash it away to be recycled by Gaia into something *better*.

If you like this kind of, umm, *shit,* then feel free to take it further with a little …

SUNSHINE UP YOUR ASS!

Ahhhhh …. Sunshine up Your Ass. Apollo's Cock, The Ronald Reagan—all are suitable names for this silly magical rite.

This is a fun spell to do after the Witchy Baptism (although, as noted, both can be done separately as well). Since I tend to do one after the other, I'll pick up where I left off with the previous spell: now fully purged from the Witchy Baptism and thoroughly sillyfied from the experience I find a nice open area, preferably a hill or large rock of some kind, crouch over, and stick my ass high into the (derri)-air. I take that glorious sunshine right up my rear! I'll sing random songs about having sunshine up my ass or getting laid by Apollo, Reaganomics, the Cold War— all are fair game! I think about all the sunshiny goodness I am taking in after having purged all that negativity during the Witchy Baptism.

Sunshine up Your Ass can be done in your own back yard on a sunny day! It can be done solo or with a best friend or intimate partner.

It is Sunshine up Your Ass!

It should be shared!

.12.

Cosmic Orgy in a Mason Jar

Mystery of the magic potion

The following is the myth that accompanies one of several potions that I concoct. For educational purposes, I will also reprint the ingredients and instructions here. This potion is *very* strong. Do not make it (and especially don't take it!) with impunity.

(Not very)secret formula

Cookware:

16 ounce Mason jar and lid (Brothel of the Cosmic Orgy).

Food thermometer (Transmutation Reader).

Cooking pan and stove (Chamber of the Sun).

Pot of water (Poseidon).

Oven (The Underworld).

Ingredients:

>One ounce of cannabis (Circe).
>Half ounce of mushrooms (Hera).
>Half gram of mandrake leaves/root (Aphrodite).
>Half gram of henbane leaves/roots/both (Hecate).
>4 cups of grain alcohol (Dionysus).

▽

Each of the four sacred plants and alcohol correspond to a different divinity: mushrooms for Hera, goddess of unity and community (*dea sodalitarum*), so that the potion may harm none; cannabis for Circe, goddess of alchemy and transformations (*dea transmutatiæ*), so that we use the potion magically to achieve our best selves through the shadow side; mandrake for Aphrodite, goddess of love (*dæmore*) because the world could always use more love; henbane for Hecate, goddess of all witches (*dea llamiarum*) because Hecate goddess of all witches; the alcohol represents Dionysus, god of intoxicated revelry (*deo enthusiasmos*). Through the five (the four sacred plants and the alcohol base) we create the Quintessence, the Fifth Element, the Psychedelic Secret, the Pocula Erotica, the Magic Potion.

Because I am sharing this potion with you, I am only suggesting a small amount of the two solanaceae ingredients, henbane and mandrake (about half a gram

117

each). The reason for this has to do with the heavy soporific effects (and lucid dreaming) that follows a large dose of solanaceae plants. The last time I made this potion a friend of mine drank it and we couldn't wake him up for about 15 hours – and this was at a party! So, if you aren't used to the effects of henbane and mandrake, they can be used in finger-pinched amounts to symbolize Hecate (henbane) and Aphrodite (mandrake).

Hecate, Aphrodite, Hera, and Dionysus are to bed each other in a Cosmic Orgy. The Cosmic Orgy should take place in the Brothel of that same name, which will then be placed on your altar. Sing to the Cosmic Orgy that night. Any song will do. Let the Orgy commence for one and a half to two weeks, shaking up the Brothel for a few seconds whenever you think about it/walk by your altar. The longer you let the Cosmic Orgy go on, the more powerful the potion will be.

But what of Circe?!

PREPARING CIRCE FOR HER SOJOURN TO THE UNDERWORLD

To fully transform into a higher state sometimes means tearing oneself apart—in other words, transforming to a lower state. As the Goddess of Alchemy and Transformations, Circe must first be torn apart so she may enter the Underworld and grow more powerful. And as we have learned to temper our egos, so Circe must acquire this lesson as well. While some prefer a coffee grinder to serrate Circe, I feel that using one's hands to shred her to pieces always has the most magical impact. Once she lies in tatters, place Circe across a flat cooking pan, as evenly as possible.

Set the Underworld to 325 degrees; once it reaches that temperature, allow Circe to descend. Do not leave her in there long—set a timer for five minutes. She should brown a little—a sign of her growing strength. She has been decarboxylated—drawing out the transformation magic deep inside her![1]

Now ascended to a higher form, Circe may join the Cosmic Orgy; for she now holds the power to transform it. This Orgy must now be overseen by Apollo, the sun god, in order to smelt all five sacred ingredients into the Quintessence.

CHAMBER OF THE SUN

We are now ready to prepare the sacred chamber (which is just nerdy magical talk for making a double-boiler and putting it on a stove ☺).

1. Take a cooking pan and fill it near to the brim with water and place on the Sun.

2. Make a "double-boiler," by using the lid of a large Mason jar (a flat, stone coffee table coaster works too) as a platform to keep the Cosmic Orgy off the

---

.1 Also, your kitchen is going to smell fabulous!

surface of the pan itself. The Brothel of the Cosmic Orgy must not be put directly on the pan.

3. Put the transmutation reader in the Brothel of the Cosmic Orgy and place it in the Chamber of the Sun.

4. Ignite the Sun at a small, slow burn.

5. Have Poseidon ready to refill the Chamber as Apollo evaporates it.

6. Stir the Cosmic Orgy every hour on the hour.

7. After about three hours the temperature will hover around 145-150 degrees. Remove the Brothel from the Chamber of the Sun and return to altar. Fumigate with incense. Sing.

8. Cover and let sit overnight.

9. Repeat the cooking process the next day by returning the Brothel of the Cosmic Orgy to the Chamber of the Sun. This time, let the Cosmic Orgy heat up to 165 degrees (takes about 4-5 hours). Set a timer for twenty minutes and monitor the temperature, adjusting as needed, to keep the Cosmic Orgy bubbling between 165 – 170 degrees otherwise you'll burn up the potion.[2] The Brothel will start to shake and the potion will bubble—clear

---

2. This will not be difficult if you let the Cosmic Orgy cook slowly, overtime.

indications that the Cosmic Orgy has intensified! This is the moment when Dionysus surrenders and merges fully with Hera, Aphrodite, Circe, and Hecate, creating the Quintessence. For just as Circe had to enter the Underworld to burn in its flames and achieve a higher state of being, Dionysus must sacrifice himself to his brother, Apollo the sun god, lose his power (evaporating the alcohol to its base), and be born again.

10. After keeping the Orgy between 165-170 degrees for twenty minutes remove the Brothel from the Chamber of the Sun and let cool down. If the potion has a light yellowish brown glycerin color it is not ready. It should look like a dirty witchy-greenish brown color.

11. Cover it, and put it back on your altar.

12. Sing to it. And let sit one night.

13. Enjoy! ☺

This is a VERY strong potion, so please approach using it carefully. Start with a small dose (about half an eye drop's worth) and wait an hour or so. I like to take it with a half pint of a good IPA.

.13.

𝒥URN IT INTO MAGIC
THE GLORIOUS END OF THIS SILLY SPELLBOOK!

Through the passage of time, the rise and fall of empires, for better or worse, we ended up here today. Psychedelics, used throughout human history in countless civilizations, have meant many things to many peoples depending on their historical and cultural circumstances. Perhaps our mission is not to use psychedelics solely to transcend reality and "drop out" of society, but rather to bring the subtle insights of the Otherworld back into our daily lives and make things better for us all. Or maybe it should just be up to each individual to choose for her, their, or himself.

There truly is magic everywhere because there are people everywhere and people hold a natural bond with the Realm of Possibility!

If taking your microdose every morning provides you with all the benefits and satisfaction you desire, all well and good! But if you are interested in receiving all the benefits and satisfaction that mushrooms (and other psychedelics) desire to give, that takes magical awareness. And every one of us has the ability for magical awareness. But as occult artist Orlee Stewart, the Mother of Abominations herself, once quipped, "magic is a muscle."[1] The more you exercise it the more you will see how it works. Hopefully, this short pamphlet of my silly little witchy ways will find some use beyond merely reading. I hope it has instead helped you consider just how magical you are and how your mind is the greatest playground ever evolved. With regard to the Three Spiritual Forces that makes up the Four Gifts, each of the spells contained herein was designed to get one or more of them stimulated and in right relation with the others. Then, you need only take Action and create your life.

Ordinary roads seldom lead to extraordinary places. The power of microdosing magic is its ability to help even the most reluctant among us rediscover the wonder of life, and therefore own our tiny slice of cosmic perspective. Indeed, such light is our inheritance from all creation. Have the courage to strive for the impossible; for when you do,

1. Orlee Andromedae, "Ars Goetia and Art," presented at Burning Star Oasis, 12, June,16.

the possible becomes reasonable.

Validate yourself, goddamn it! Recognize your magic. Align your Four Gifts and swim comfortably in the enchanted Ocean that is the Realm of Possibility.

Once you do, life blossoms into a magical mindgasm.

And when that happens, miracles aren't necessary.

Welcome to the Psychedelic Renaissance.

☺

$\mathcal{B}$IBLIOGRAPHY

Andromedae, Orlee. "Ars Goetia and Art," presented at Burning Star Oasis, 12, June, 16.

Austin, Paul. *Microdosing Psychedelics: A Practical Guide to Upgrade Your Life* (Amazon Digital Services, 2018).

Desai, Ashwin and Goolam Vahed, *The South African Gandhi: Stretcher-Bearer of Empire* (CA: Stanford University Press, 2015).

Dobkin de Rios, Marlene and Oscar Janiger, *LSD: Spirituality and the Creative Process* (VT: Park Street Press, 2003).

Ellis, Robert M. *The Trouble with Buddhism* (Lulu.com, 2011).

IAO 131, *Naturalistic Occultism: An Introduction to Scientific Illuminism* (Society of Scientific Illuminism, 2012).

Harris, Sam. *Waking Up: A Guide to Spirituality Without Religion* (NY: Simon and Schuster, 2014).

Hoffman, Bob. *No One is to Blame: Freedom from Compulsive Self-Defeating Behavior* (CA: Recycling Books, 1988).

Kilham, Chris. "Not All Visions are Wise," presented at Spirit Plant Medicine Conference, 4, November, 17.

Letcher, Andy. *Shroom: A Cultural History of the Magic Mushroom* (Harper Perennial, 2008).
Minor Anthologies of the Pali Canon, Part III.

Mori, K., et. al. "Effects of Hericium erinaceus on amyloid β (25-35) peptide-induced learning and memory deficits in mice" in *Biomedical Research* 2009, 32(1).

Mori et. al., "Improving effects of the mushroom Yamabushitake (Hericium erinaceus) on mild cognitive impairment: a double-blind placebo-controlled clinical trial," in *Phytotherapy Research*, March 2009;23(3).

O' Neel, Karen. "Beating Bulimia with Ibogaine,"

presented for the Portland Psychedelic Society, 10, May, 2018.

Ott, Jonathan (trans.). Albert Hofmann, *LSD: My Problem Child* (LA: JP Tarcher Inc., 1983).

Owens, Gale R., *Rites and Religions of the Anglo-Saxons* (David and Charles: Barnes and Noble, 1981).

Pike, Eunice V. and Florence Cowan, "Mushroom Ritual verses Christianity" in *Practical Anthropology*, Vol. 6, No. 4 (July-August 1959).

— "Mazatec Sexual Impurity and Bible Reading," in *Practical Anthropology*, Volume 7 (2).

Reynolds, Richard D. *Cry for War: The Story of Suzan and Michael Carson* (CA: Walnut Creek, Squibob Press, 1987).

Sessa, Ben. *The Psychedelic Renaissance: Reassessing the Role of Psychedelic Drugs in 21st Century Psychiatry and Society* (UK: Muswell Hill Press, 2012).

Tannahill, Reay. *Food in History* (UK: Eyre Methuen, 1973).

Wooster, David et. al. *Pacific Medical Journal* Vol. 47, No. 1 (Jan., 1904).

Hawkeye Clark, pers. comm.

Jonathan Thompson, pers. comm.

blog.bulletproof.com.

businessinsider.com.

erowid.org.

ft.com.

mycotopia.net.

thethirdwave.co.

wired.co.uk.

Made in the USA
Middletown, DE
22 May 2020